COMMON

COMMON GROUND

AN ANTHOLOGY
SELECTED BY

Marghanita Laski

CARCANET

First published in 1989 by
Carcanet Press Limited
208-212 Corn Exchange Buildings
Manchester M4 3BQ

British Library Cataloguing in Publication Data

Laski, Marghanita, *1915-1988*
    The common reader.
    I. Title   C c
    821'.914

    ISBN 0-85635-800-2

6003641899

The publisher acknowledges financial assistance from
the Arts Council of Great Britain

Set in 10½pt Palatino by Bryan Williamson, Darwen, Lancashire
Printed and bound in England by SRP Ltd, Exeter

Acknowledgements

The author and publishers wish to thank the following who have kindly given permission for the use of copyright material.

Jonathan Cape Ltd. on behalf of the Estate of Robert Frost with Henry Holt and Company, Inc. for 'Stopping by Woods on a Snowy Evening', 'Mending Wall' and 'The Runaway' from *The Poetry of Robert Frost*, ed. Edward Connery Lathem. Copyright 1923, 1930 by Holt, Rinehart and Winston and renewed 1951, 1958 by Robert Frost; and on behalf of the Executors of the W.H. Davies Estate with Wesleyan University Press for 'Leisure' and 'A Child's Pet' from *The Complete Poems of W.H. Davies*. Copyright 1963 by Jonathan Cape Ltd.

Century Hutchinson Publishing Group Ltd. for 'Parting in Wartime' from *Collected Poems* by Frances Cornford.

Curtis Brown Group Ltd. on behalf of the Estate of Vita Sackville-West for 'The Greater Cats' by Vita Sackville-West, Hogarth Press; and 'Family Court' by Ogden Nash. Copyright © Ogden Nash.

Gerald Duckworth and Company Ltd. with Viking Penguin Inc. for 'Pictures in the Smoke' from *The Portable Dorothy Parker* by Dorothy Parker. Copyright © 1927, renewed 1955 by Dorothy Parker.

The Estate of Norma Millay Ellis for 'First Fig' and 'Dirge Without Music' by Edna St Vincent Millay from *Collected Poems*, Harper and Row. Copyright © 1922, 1928, 1950, 1955 by Edna St Vincent Millay and Norma Millay Ellis.

Faber and Faber Ltd. with Macmillan Publishing Company for 'Silence' by Marianne Moore from *Collected Poems* and *The Complete Poems of Marianne Moore*. Copyright © 1935 by Marianne Moore, renewed 1963 by Marianne Moore and T.S. Eliot; and with Random House, Inc. for Epilogue from 'The Orators'. Copyright 1934 and renewed 1962 by W.H. Auden, and 'September 1, 1939'. Copyright © 1940 by W.H. Auden, from *Collected Poems* and *The English Auden: Poems, Essays and Dramatic Writings* by W.H. Auden, ed. Edward Mendelson.

David Higham Associates Ltd. and New Directions Publishing Corporation for 'Do not go gentle into that good night' by Dylan Thomas from *Poems of Dylan Thomas* and *The Poems*, Dent. Copyright © 1952 by Dylan Thomas; and 'For Johnny' by John Pudney from *Collected Poems*, Putnam & Co.

James MacGibbon, Executor of the Estate of Stevie Smith, for 'The Galloping Cat' and 'Not Waving but Drowning' from *The Collected Poems of Stevie Smith*, Penguin Modern Classics.

Macmillan Publishers Ltd. and St. Martins Press, Inc. for 'The Bells of Heaven' and 'Time, you old gipsy man' from *Collected Poems* by Ralph Hodgson. Copyright © 1961 by Ralph Hodgson.

Peters Fraser and Dunlop Ltd. for 'Tarantella', 'Ha'nacker Mill' and 'On a Sleeping Friend' from *Sonnets and Verse* by Hilaire Belloc, Gerald Duck-

Contents

Beliefs and Doubts

Moralities

Home

Distances

Open Air

Poor Beasts

Plain Tales

Signs of the Times

Gone for a Soldier

Accidie

Time Passing

Deaths and Endings

Introduction

Perhaps this collection should have been called Common Ground
Three. Certainly there are two that should go before it, though
neither in a book. The first is the collection of rhymes, sayings
and superstitions that we learn almost as soon as we learn any-
thing at all, go on learning for at least the first part of our lives,
and carry with us as long as our memories last. Common Ground
Two is words with tunes. To some extent it overlaps with One:
'Bye Baby Bunting' has a tune, 'Ring-a-ring-of-roses' has a tune.
But the songs of Common Ground Two are not only the baby
songs but the songs that most of us know, songs that go with us
all through life: the so-called folksongs, a name that usually
means no more than that the song's maker has been forgotten,
as with 'Greensleeves' and 'The Derby Ram'; the popular songs
whose makers *are* known, like 'John Peel' and 'The Lambeth
Walk'; the hymns and carols, the Victorian music-hall songs, the
First World War songs, patriotic songs and revolutionary songs
and wicked songs set to old tunes that everyone knows – there
are always more words than tunes – and love-songs, whether old
love-songs that seem to have gone on for ever, or whatever happen
to be the best-remembered love-songs of our own wooing days.

Common Ground Three is the poetry you will find in this book.
For centuries, the first two common uses of words, with and
without music, have been so much a part of our common ground
that we could simply take them for granted, without having to
think about them. Now in the last decades of the twentieth cen-
tury, we must.

It is true that with the dislocations of industrial revolutions and
war and ever more rapid class-changes, much of our native cul-
ture may be a bit shaky. But it is an astonishingly tough and
resilient culture, and we are very responsive to it, not only
remembering an enormous pack of the old words and tunes, but
forever picking up new words, rhymes and catch-phrases from
no matter where, though mostly North America – 'Stop the
world, I want to get off!' 'Laughing all the way to the bank'
'Thank heaven for little girls!' – and tunes like (I myself hate this
one) 'Happy birthday to you!' To have the common ground of
these words and tunes and rituals, as appropriate to our age and
class and group and occasion, is to share the common culture
that makes us English.

I do not know about other nations, but it is certain that the
English have a constant need for that rhythmical and usually

rhyming use of language which we call poetry, good and bad. Almost all the childish uses of language of Common Ground One are poetry, much of it good poetry. All the songs of Common Ground Two are, in this general sense, poetry. So are the advertising jingles and dirty limericks which amuse so many adults. In fact, adults use poetry, usually rather poor poetry, in far more places than we are generally aware of: on greetings cards and on condolence cards, and in the death columns of many local papers, where suitable stocks of poetry are kept for the bereaved to choose from. Yet why, you may ask, when we have the richest language in the world and the richest poetry in the world, do most people use trash for poetry when in need of it? I think the answer is that for too long most people have been more or less deliberately cut off from the common culture, and that none of the reasons for this is commendable or palatable.

Some ten years ago we celebrated, or were supposed to celebrate, something called National Poetry Year. Most people didn't notice it. The BBC did, and sent a television reporter into the London streets to stop people at random and ask them if they could say any poetry by heart. Two people only were able to recite poems: a white man (I forget his poem) and a black woman who started in on Poe's 'The Raven' and could clearly have gone on to the end. A few people said '"I wandered lonely as a cloud –" but I don't remember any more and I don't know who wrote it'. No one offered an advertising jingle, so clearly they distinguished this kind of rhyme from 'poetry'. Many, many people said they had been put off poetry at school. In many schools poetry is unattractively taught by teachers who themselves have no response to it or, if they have, cannot communicate it. Sometimes they do not want to. There are teachers who regard the common ground of English poetry as reeking of upper-class culture and unsuited to the egalitarian society for which they want to prepare their pupils.

In one respect at least they could be right. Until I came to choose poems for this collection, I had not realized to how great an extent much of the best English poetry rests upon the very limited common ground of a classical education. Take, for instance, this four-line poem written in the early nineteenth century by Walter Savage Landor:

> Stand close around, ye Stygian set,
>> With Dirce in one boat conveyed!
> Or Charon, seeing, may forget
>> That he is old, and she a shade.

Without a classical education, this good poem is inaccessible. Few people today have such an education, even to the extent of reading or hearing the classical myths and legends, which could open up to them this huge, rich tract of English poetry. My collection is intended to be almost entirely accessible. What cannot be easily guessed or looked up I leave out. So once in a way, when a classical reference seems clear in its context, I have let it in. But the loss, in general, of classical lore is a great loss to poetry-readers, and not least because this is a loss of names – names, resonant, echoing, evocative, essential to poetry.

It is certain that what applies to classical education applies to a sadly large extent to Christian education too. Here is the last verse of a poem written during the early years of the First World War, which the Americans had then decided to stay out of, being, as their President Wilson had said, 'Too proud to fight':

> Brethren, how must it fare with me
>   Or how am I justified,
> If it be proven that I am he
>   For whom mankind has died –
> If it be proven that I am he
>   Who, being questioned, denied?

In only some seventy years I dare say this verse has become incomprehensible except to members of strict Calvinist sects, perhaps only to Scots. However, there are still more practising Christians than classicists in Britain, and I have let in a good many poems of Christian and/or Biblical reference in the belief (or perhaps only the hope) that they will be open to many readers still.

That last verse was from a poem by Rudyard Kipling, and he provides a good example of the ways that teachers may hinder pupils' responses to poetry. Kipling is the greatest popular poet England has yet had. If most of his work has depth under depth to be plumbed, most of his poetry is, on the surface, easily reachable, and, more, speaks aloud most excellently in dialect voices.

Time, wrote the poet W.H. Auden – in his epitaph for the Irish writer W.B. Yeats – time worships language and forgives everyone who lives by it:

> Time that with this strange excuse
>   Pardoned Kipling and his views,
> And will pardon Paul Claudel,
>   Pardons him for writing well.

But time has not yet pardoned Kipling, as it has pardoned

Shakespeare, whose own views were at least as 'right-wing', and in days when the 'left-wing' views of the Levellers (in many ways like today's extreme left views) were available for him to embrace. But Shakespeare is far enough away for forgiveness even by the doctrinaire. Kipling is not. Few people today seem able to accept art, at least the art of words, unless they approve not only the sentiments in the works but the private views of the maker too. So Kipling, the poet through whom poetry could, probably, be most easily brought to children at school, is often withheld from them.

For much of poetry's inaccessibility to people today the BBC must be blamed, though heaven knows it has, by its lights, tried to do right by poetry. But most of its lights are of the wrong wattage. The upper-class voices in which almost all poetry is introduced and read, the 'putting in the expression' (often wrongly), the patronizing comments of the presenter, are enough to put off from poetry anyone who hasn't already been put off at school. (I have to add that, very occasionally, the BBC has given us poems read superbly; and that they have let me present several programmes of Kipling's poetry read in appropriate, not only genteel voices.)

The last reason I shall give for the common lack of familiarity with good poetry is one for which I blame the Arts Council and similar, often associated, bodies. During the years I was at the Arts Council, no money was spent on poetry that did not benefit living poets. Now I do not condemn the work of living poets in saying that very little of it is immediately, easily accessible. To suggest only one reason for this, most of it is written in the forms that used to be called prose poems or free verse, not in the rhyming, rhythmical shapes that make an immediate appeal. But if the Arts Council really wanted to increase knowledge and appreciation and understanding of poetry they would have been considering how they might bring to the public accessible poems, by definition mostly older poems, from the great English store. To support a few little magazines for new work to appear in is right – so long as no magazine is supported for so long that it becomes an institution or a pet. To pay poets to read their own work aloud, to reside in or visit institutions where they can teach people to write passable prose poems is, to my mind, a waste of public money. It is easy to teach anyone to write what looks like a passable prose poem, and then to over-praise it. For it seems to be very difficult indeed for anyone, even a professional critic, to know whether rhymeless, rhythmless poems are any good or not. Certainly they are hard to come close to, and do not slip naturally into the memory.

In Common Ground Three, whether this collection of mine or the body of English poetry from which it is drawn, all poems have marked rhythm and usually rhyme. And as it turns out, and not by deliberate choice, many of the poems here have almost the simplest of rhyming forms: a four-line verse in which the second and fourth lines rhyme with each other, and sometimes the first and the third as well. These rhyming shapes for poetry are very old, and they are not natively English. From about 700 AD, the English (or, as they were then, the Anglo-Saxons) wrote their poetry in long lines of alliterative verse, and there were no rhymes. Each line had three or four words beginning with the same letter, or nearly the same sound, and the poetry was spoken aloud by a professional bard, with heavy stress on these words. Here, for example, are the first two lines of the famous Anglo-Saxon poem *Beowulf*, translated into modern English by Michael Alexander: 'We have heard of the *th*riving of the *th*rone of *D*enmark, / how the *f*olk-kings *f*lourished in *f*ormer days...'

But on the Continent, the kind of poetry we know best today, the rhythmical, rhyming poetry, was already the common form. At this date it was almost entirely written in Vulgar Latin, the spoken Latin which was the common language of educated Christendom. In 1929 the English scholar Helen Waddell made some fine translations of some of these Latin poems, using almost the shapes and rhythms of the originals. Here is a verse from what she called 'the greatest drinking song in the world', by one of those wandering scholars who roamed around Europe in the early Middle Ages:

> Down the broad way do I go
>   Young and unregretting,
> Wrap me in my vices up,
>   Virtue all forgetting,
> Greedier for all delight
>   Than heaven to enter in:
> Since the soul in me is dead,
>   Better save the skin.

If I had not revealed this as originally a Latin poem, it could certainly pass for native English, and once the Conquest had opened England up to a wider Christendom, this kind of poetry soon became our common form, at least in the South of England. In the North, the old alliterative form lasted long enough for Chaucer to make fun of it in the *Canterbury Tales*: 'I am a Southren man, I cannot tell a tale in "rum, ram, ruf" by letter', says his Parson. While Chaucer, at the end of the fourteenth century, was writing with equal polish in English (by then the language of Parliament), in French (still used by the educated upper classes), and in Latin (still the European common language), away up in Cheshire a poet whose name we don't know was writing the last of the great alliterative poems. Yet this, *Sir Gawain and the Green Knight*, already ended each of its sections with a little four-line verse in the all-conquering rhyming poetry. The alliterative verse died out, though it has influenced a few later poets: W.H. Auden was one. What will happen to the twentieth-century's overwhelming preference for prose poetry we must wait and see.

None of the poems in this book is here because it ought to be here. This is not meant for a collection of representative English poetry, but of *useful* English poetry for people who may have missed out on this part of their inheritance, but who have, as I believe, a natural inclination to look for poetry in extreme situations: in extreme grief, in extreme joy, when confronting love or fear or natural beauty. Poetry is like magic, lifting us out of ourselves into states strange and exalted. 'To spell' meant and can still mean to use words to enchant. 'Grammar' once meant magic itself. The only criterion for a poem being here is that I have found it magical, and easy to get hold of, and therefore useful; I expect that other people will too.

There are three main ways we can get and keep hold of poetry. One is by hearing it. I have already indicated that listening to poetry can do more harm than good, unless the reading is itself one of near genius. There are such readings. I remember hearing on the radio Peggy Ashcroft read Emily Brontë's poems, the war-blinded poet Esmond Percy, read Chesterton's 'Lepanto', Eleanor Bron reading Tennyson's 'Enoch Arden'. But do not believe anyone who tells you that poems are meant to be read aloud. People who say this are usually people who profit from poems being read aloud. Hardly any serious poems written since the Renaissance are meant for reading aloud, apart from modern prose poems.

The second way to take in a poem is to read it to yourself. This is a good and right way. The third is to know it by heart, so as to have it immediately in mind when you need it. There is no poem here of which I do not know some or most or all of by heart, and this is not by setting out to learn them. It is either by reading them so often that I can't help but know them, or by copying them into a commonplace book. The advice to keep a commonplace book was one of the best things I got out of the Manchester school that I left when I was thirteen. If you keep a notebook in which you copy out anything that strikes you as valuable and add to it the date you did this, you will soon have a good word collection of your own and a good reflection of your own changing tastes; and you will discover, willy-nilly, that you have got a lot of its contents by heart.

I ought to add a few comments on the selection and arrangement in this book. Because *Common Ground* may be many people's first poetry book, the poems are generally printed in modern English, except for a few in modified Scots-English. And that there are only a few poems from the fine body of Scots poetry is because of the language difficulty. This is, first and foremost, an English anthology.

I have not included any words of songs where you think of the tune as soon as you hear the words, because to know the tune alters the way you say the words. For instance, in the carol 'The Holly and the Ivy', you will space and stress the words to the echoing tune.

I readily admit that many poems here could be in another section than the one in which I have put them, but these possibilities are what we should expect. The titles of some poems are mine, not the poets'. You may think this impertinent, but there are often good reasons for doing it. The poem I have called 'Cynara' was titled by the poet 'Non sum qualis eram bonae sub regno Cynarae'; the reason for renaming it is clear. Sometimes a new title saves a note, for instance, calling Allan Cunningham's poem 'The Homesick Jacobite' rather than 'It's hame and it's hame'.

Finally, a note about possibly surprising omissions. Great poems and great poets there are indeed not represented here: there is nothing by Edmund Spenser, only two poems by John Donne, and only two lines by Alexander Pope. The reason is that most of these poets' works are accessible only to people who have become used to poetry, have discovered that there is much in English poetry to which their pulse beats in response. All the poems in this book have at one time or another worked in this way for me. There is no poem that I have not at some time – and of course our needs change from time to time – found magical and useful and easy to get hold of.

Marghanita Laski was working on *Common Ground* at the time of her death. The assembly of the text was completed, following her instructions as closely as possible, by Mark Fisher.

Loves

My Love is like a Red Red Rose

My love is like a red red rose
   That's newly sprung in June:
My love is like the melodie
   That's sweetly play'd in tune.

So fair art thou, my bonnie lass,
   So deep in love am I:
And I will love thee still, my dear,
   Till a' the seas gang dry.

Till a' the seas gang dry, my dear,
   And the rocks melt wi' the sun:
And I will love thee still, my dear,
   While the sands o' life shall run.

And fare thee weel, my only love,
   And fare thee weel awhile!
And I will come again, my love,
   Tho' it were ten thousand mile.

ROBERT BURNS

Jenny Kiss'd Me

Jenny kiss'd me when we met,
   Jumping from the chair she sat in;
Time, you thief, who love to get
   Sweets into your list, put that in!
Say I'm weary, say I'm sad,
   Say that health and wealth have miss'd me,
Say I'm growing old, but add,
     Jenny kiss'd me.

LEIGH HUNT

So We'll Go No More A-roving

So we'll go no more a-roving
  So late into the night,
Though the heart be still as loving,
  And the moon be still as bright.

For the sword outwears its sheath,
  And the soul wears out the breast,
And the heart must pause to breathe,
  And Love itself have rest.

Though the night was made for loving,
  And the day returns too soon,
Yet we'll go no more a-roving
  By the light of the moon.

GEORGE GORDON, LORD BYRON

When You Are Old

When you are old and grey and full of sleep,
And nodding by the fire, take down this book,
And slowly read, and dream of the soft look
Your eyes had once, and of their shadows deep;

How many loved your moments of glad grace,
And loved your beauty with love false or true,
But one man loved the pilgrim soul in you,
And loved the sorrows of your changing face;

And bending down beside the glowing bars,
Murmur, a little sadly, how Love fled
And paced upon the mountains overhead
And hid his face amid a crowd of stars.

W.B. YEATS

Cynara

Last night, ah, yesternight, betwixt her lips and mine
There fell thy shadow, Cynara! thy breath was shed
Upon my soul between the kisses and wine;
And I was desolate and sick of an old passion,
   Yea, I was desolate and bowed my head:
I have been faithful to thee, Cynara! in my fashion.

All night upon mine heart I felt her warm heart beat,
Night-long within mine arms in love and sleep she lay;
Surely the kisses of her bought red mouth were sweet;
But I was desolate and sick of an old passion,
   When I awoke and found the dawn was gray:
I have been faithful to thee, Cynara! in my fashion.

I have forgot much, Cynara! gone with the wind,
Flung roses, roses riotously with the throng,
Dancing, to put thy pale, lost lilies out of mind;
But I was desolate and sick of an old passion,
   Yea, all the time, because the dance was long:
I have been faithful to thee, Cynara! in my fashion.

I cried for madder music and for stronger wine,
But when the feast is finished and the lamps expire,
Then falls thy shadow, Cynara! the night is thine;
And I am desolate and sick of an old passion,
   Yea hungry for the lips of my desire:
I have been faithful to thee, Cynara! in my fashion.

ERNEST DOWSON

The Vampire

A fool there was and he made his prayer
   (Even as you and I!)
To a rag and a bone and a hank of hair
(We called her the woman who did not care)
But the fool he called her his lady fair –
   (Even as you and I!)

Oh, the years we waste and the tears we waste
And the work of our head and hand
Belong to the woman who did not know
(And now we know that she never could know)
And did not understand!

A fool there was and his goods he spent
(Even as you and I!)
Honour and faith and a sure intent
(And it wasn't the least what the lady meant)
But a fool must follow his natural bent
(Even as you and I!)

Oh, the toil we lost and the spoil we lost
And the excellent things we planned
Belong to the woman who didn't know why
(And now we know that she never knew why)
And did not understand!

The fool was stripped to his foolish hide
(Even as you and I!)
Which she might have seen when she threw him aside –
(But it isn't on record the lady tried)
So some of him lived but the most of him died –
(Even as you and I!)

And it isn't the shame and it isn't the blame
That stings like a white-hot brand –
It's coming to know that she never knew why
(Seeing, at last, she could never know why)
And never could understand!

RUDYARD KIPLING

Yasmin

How splendid in the morning glows the lily: with what grace he
    throws
His supplication to the rose: do roses nod the head, Yasmin?

But when the silver dove descends I find the little flower of friends
Whose very name that sweetly ends I say when I have said, Yasmin.

The morning light is clear and cold: I dare not in that light behold
A whiter light, a deeper gold, a glory too far shed, Yasmin.

But when the deep red eye of day is level with the lone highway,
And some to Meccah turn to pray, and I toward thy bed, Yasmin;

Or when the wind beneath the moon is drifting like a soul aswoon,
And harping planets talk love's tune with milky wings outspread,
    Yasmin,

Shower down thy love, O burning bright! For one night or the
    other night
Will come the Gardener in white, and gathered flowers are dead,
    Yasmin.

JAMES ELROY FLECKER

'O mistress mine! where are you roaming?'

O mistress mine! where are you roaming?
O! stay and hear; your true love's coming.
    That can sing both high and low.
Trip no further, pretty sweeting;
Journeys end in lovers meeting,
    Every wise man's son doth know.

What is love? 'tis not hereafter;
Present mirth hath present laughter;
    What's to come is still unsure:
In delay there lies no plenty;
Then come kiss me, sweet-and-twenty,
    Youth's a stuff will not endure.

WILLIAM SHAKESPEARE

A Leave-taking

Let us go hence, my songs; she will not hear.
Let us go hence together without fear;
Keep silence now, for singing-time is over,
And over all old things and all things dear.
She loves not you nor me as all we love her.
Yea, though we sang as angels in her ear,
        She would not hear.

Let us rise up and part; she will not know.
Let us go seaward as the great winds go,
Full of blown sand and foam; what help is here?
There is no help, for all these things are so,
And all the world is bitter as a tear.
And how these things are, though ye strove to show,
        She would not know.

Let us go home and hence; she will not weep.
We gave love many dreams and days to keep,
Flowers without scent, and fruits that would not grow,
Saying 'If thou wilt, thrust in thy sickle and reap.'
All is reaped now; no grass is left to mow;
And we that sowed, though all we fell on sleep,
        She would not weep.

Let us go hence and rest; she will not love.
She shall not hear us if we sing hereof,
Nor see love's ways, how sore they are and steep.
Come hence, let be, lie still; it is enough.
Love is a barren sea, bitter and deep;
And though she saw all heaven in flower above,
        She would not love.

Let us give up, go down; she will not care.
Though all the stars made gold of all the air,
And the sea moving saw before it move
One moon-flower making all the foam-flowers fair;
Though all those waves went over us, and drove
Deep down the stifling lips and drowning hair,
        She would not care.

Let us go hence, go hence; she will not see.
Sing all once more together; surely she,
She too, remembering days and words that were,
Will turn a little toward us, sighing; but we,
We are hence, we are gone, as though we had not been there.
Nay, and though all men seeing had pity on me,
    She would not see.

ALGERNON CHARLES SWINBURNE

Summer Night

Now sleeps the crimson petal, now the white;
Nor waves the cypress in the palace walk;
Nor winks the gold fin in the porphyry font:
The fire-fly wakens: waken thou with me.

Now droops the milkwhite peacock like a ghost,
And like a ghost she glimmers on to me.

Now lies the Earth all Danaë to the stars,
And all thy heart lies open unto me.

Now slides the silent meteor on, and leaves
A shining furrow, as thy thoughts in me.

Now folds the lily all her sweetness up,
And slips into the bosom of the lake:
So fold thyself, my dearest, thou, and slip
Into my bosom and be lost in me.

ALFRED, LORD TENNYSON

A Birthday

My heart is like a singing bird
   Whose nest is in a watered shoot:
My heart is like an apple-tree
   Whose boughs are bent with thickset fruit;
My heart is like a rainbow shell
   That paddles in a halcyon sea;
My heart is gladder than all these
   Because my love is come to me.

Raise me a dais of silk and down;
   Hang it with vair and purple dyes;
Carve it in doves and pomegranates,
   And peacocks with a hundred eyes;
Work it in gold and silver grapes,
   In leaves and silver fleur-de-lys;
Because the birthday of my life
   Is come, my love is come to me.

CHRISTINA ROSSETTI

To his Coy Mistress

Had we but world enough, and time,
This coyness, Lady, were no crime.
We would sit down, and think which way
To walk, and pass our long love's day.
Thou by the Indian Ganges' side
Shouldst rubies find: I by the tide
Of Humber would complain. I would
Love you ten years before the Flood:
And you should, if you please, refuse
Till the conversion of the Jews.
My vegetable love should grow
Vaster than Empires, and more slow;
An hundred years should go to praise
Thine eyes, and on thy forehead gaze.
Two hundred to adore each breast:
But thirty thousand to the rest.
An age at least to every part,

And the last age should show your heart.
For, Lady, you deserve this state;
Nor would I love at lower rate.
　But at my back I always hear
Time's wingèd chariot hurrying near:
And yonder all before us lie
Deserts of vast eternity.
Thy beauty shall no more be found,
Nor, in thy marble vault, shall sound
My echoing song: then worms shall try
That long-preserved virginity:
And your quaint honour turn to dust;
And into ashes all my lust.
The grave's a fine and private place,
But none I think do there embrace.
　Now therefore, while the youthful hue
Sits on thy skin like morning dew,
And while thy willing soul transpires
At every pore with instant fires,
Now let us sport us while we may;
And now, like amorous birds of prey,
Rather at once our time devour,
Than languish in his slow-chapt power.
Let us roll all our strength, and all
Our sweetness, up into one ball:
And tear our pleasures with rough strife,
Thorough the iron gates of life.
Thus, though we cannot make our sun
Stand still, yet we will make him run.

ANDREW MARVELL

O Western Wind

O Western wind, when wilt thou blow
　That the small rain down can rain?
Christ, that my love were in my arms
　And I in my bed again!

ANON

'There is a Lady sweet and kind'

There is a Lady sweet and kind,
Was never face so pleased my mind;
I did but see her passing by,
And yet I love her till I die.

Her gesture, motion, and her smiles,
Her wit, her voice, my heart beguiles,
Beguiles my heart, I know not why,
And yet I love her till I die....

Cupid is wingèd and doth range
Her country so my love doth change:
But change she earth, or change she sky,
Yet will I love her till I die.

THOMAS FORD

The Parting

Since there's no help, come let us kiss and part:
Nay, I have done; you get no more of me,
And I am glad, yea, glad with all my heart,
That thus so cleanly I myself can free;
Shake hands for ever, cancel all our vows,
And when we meet at any time again,
Be it not seen in either of our brows,
That we one jot of former love retain.
Now at the last gasp of love's latest breath,
When, his pulse failing, passion speechless lies,
When faith is kneeling by his bed of death,
And innocence is closing up his eyes,
Now, if thou wouldst, when all have given him over,
From death to life thou mightst him yet recover.

MICHAEL DRAYTON

To the Virgins, to make much of Time

Gather ye rosebuds while ye may,
  Old Time is still a flying:
And this same flower that smiles today,
  Tomorrow will be dying.

The glorious lamp of heaven, the sun,
  The higher he's a getting;
The sooner will his race be run,
  And nearer he's to setting.

That age is best, which is the first,
  When youth and blood are warmer;
But being spent, the worse, and worst
  Times, still succeed the former.

Then be not coy, but use your time;
  And while ye may, go marry:
For having lost but once your prime,
  You may for ever tarry.

ROBERT HERRICK

To Lucasta, Going to the Wars

Tell me not (Sweet) I am unkind,
  That from the nunnery
Of thy chaste breast, and quiet mind,
  To war and arms I fly.

True; a new mistress now I chase,
  The first foe in the field;
And with a stronger faith embrace
  A sword, a horse, a shield.

Yet this inconstancy is such,
  As you too shall adore;
I could not love thee (Dear) so much,
  Loved I not honour more.

RICHARD LOVELACE

The Night has a Thousand Eyes

The night has a thousand eyes,
   And the day but one;
Yet the light of the bright world dies
   With the dying sun.

The mind has a thousand eyes,
   And the heart but one;
Yet the light of a whole life dies
   When love is done.

F.W. BOURDILLON

'My Love in her attire doth show her wit'

My Love in her attire doth show her wit,
   It doth so well become her:
For every season she hath dressings fit,
   For Winter, Spring, and Summer.
No beauty she doth miss
When all her robes are on:
But Beauty's self she is
When all her robes are gone.

ANON

John Anderson my jo

John Anderson my jo, John,
   When we were first acquent,
Your locks were like the raven,
   Your bonnie brow was brent;
But now your brow is beld, John,
   Your locks are like the snow;
But blessings on your frosty pow,
   John Anderson, my jo.

34

John Anderson my jo, John,
  We clamb the hill the gither;
And mony a canty day, John,
  We've had wi' ane anither:
Now we maun totter down, John,
  And hand in hand we'll go,
And sleep the gither at the foot,
  John Anderson, my jo.

ROBERT BURNS

The Passionate Shepherd to his Love

Come live with me, and be my love,
And we will all the pleasures prove
That valleys, groves, hills and fields,
Woods, or steepy mountain yields.

And we will sit upon the rocks,
Seeing the shepherds feed their flocks
By shallow rivers, to whose falls
Melodious birds sing madrigals.

And I will make thee beds of roses,
And a thousand fragrant posies,
A cap of flowers, and a kirtle,
Embroidered all with leaves of myrtle.

A gown made of the finest wool
Which from our pretty lambs we pull,
Fair linèd slippers for the cold,
With buckles of the purest gold.

A belt of straw and ivy-buds,
With coral clasps and amber studs,
And if these pleasures may thee move,
Come live with me, and be my love.

The shepherd swains shall dance and sing
For thy delight each May morning.
If these delights thy mind may move,
Then live with me, and be my love.

CHRISTOPHER MARLOWE

The Bait

Come live with me and be my love,
And we will some new pleasures prove,
Of golden sands and crystal brooks,
With silken lines and silver hooks.

There will the river whispering run,
Warmed by thine eyes more than the sun;
And there th' enamoured fish will stay,
Begging themselves they may betray.

When thou wilt swim in that live bath,
Each fish, which every channel hath,
Will amorously to thee swim,
Gladder to catch thee than thou him.

If thou to be so seen beest loth
By sun or moon, thou dark'nest both;
And if myself have leave to see,
I need not their light, having thee.

Let others freeze with angling reeds,
And cut their legs with shells and weeds,
Or treacherously poor fish beset
With strangling snare, or windowy net:

Let coarse bold hands from slimy nest
The bedded fish in banks out-wrest,
Or curious traitors, sleave-silk flies
Bewitch poor fishes' wand'ring eyes.

For thee, thou need'st no such deceit,
For thou thyself art thine own bait;
That fish that is not catched thereby,
Alas, is wiser far than I.

JOHN DONNE

Sonnet 129

The expense of spirit in a waste of shame
Is lust in action; and till action, lust
Is perjured, murderous, bloody, full of blame,
Savage, extreme, rude, cruel, not to trust;
Enjoy'd no sooner but despised straight;
Past reason hunted; and no sooner had,
Past reason hated, as a swallowed bait,
On purpose laid to make the taker mad:
Mad in pursuit, and in possession so;
Had, having, and in quest to have, extreme;
A bliss in proof, and proved, a very woe;
Before, a joy proposed; behind, a dream.
    All this the world well knows; yet none knows well
    To shun the heaven that leads men to this hell.

WILLIAM SHAKESPEARE

Pictures in the Smoke

Oh, gallant was the first love, and glittering and fine;
    The second love was water, in a clear white cup;
The third love was his, and the fourth was mine;
    And after that, I always get them all mixed up.

DOROTHY PARKER

Lament of the Maister of Erskine

Depart, depart, depart,
Allace! I must depart
From her that has my heart,
     With heart full sore,
Against my will indeed,
And can find no remeid:
I wait the pains of deid
     Can do no more.

Now must I go, allace!
From sicht of her sweet face,
The grund of all my grace,
     And sovereign;
What chance that may fall me,
Sall I never merry be,
Unto the time I see
     My sweet again.

I go, and wait nocht where,
I wander here and there,
I weep and sighs richt sair
     With painis smart;
Now must I pass away, away,
In wilderness and wilsum way,
Allace! this woeful day
     We suld depart.

My spreit does quake for dreid,
My thirlit hairt does bleed,
My painis does exceed –
     What suld I say?
I, woeful wicht, alone,
Makand ane piteous moan,
Allace! my hairt is gone
     For ever and ay.

Through langour of my sweet
So thirlit is my spreit,
My days are most complete
     Through her absence;

Christ! sen she knew my smert,
Ingravit in my hairt,
Because I must depairt
  From her presence.

Adieu, my awin sweet thing,
My joy and comforting,
My mirth and solacing
  Of erdly gloir!
Fareweill, my lady bricht,
And my remembrance richt;
Fareweill and have guid nicht:
  I say no more.

ALEXANDER SCOTT

Dreams and Fantasies

A Lyke-Wake Dirge

This ae nighte, this ae nighte,
  — *Every nighte and alle,*
Fire and fleet and candle-lighte,
  And Christe receive thy saule.

When thou from hence away art past,
  — *Every nighte and alle,*
To Whinny-muir thou com'st at last;
  And Christe receive thy saule.

If ever thou gavest hosen and shoon,
  — *Every nighte and alle,*
Sit thee down and put them on;
  And Christe receive thy saule.

If hosen and shoon thou ne'er gav'st nane
  — *Every nighte and alle,*
The whinnes sall prick thee to the bare bane;
  And Christe receive thy saule.

From Whinny-muir when thou may'st pass,
  — *Every nighte and alle,*
To Brig o' Dread thou com'st at last;
  And Christe receive thy saule.

From Brig o' Dread when thou may'st pass,
  — *Every nighte and alle,*
To Purgatory fire thou com'st at last;
  And Christe receive thy saule.

If ever thou gavest meat or drink,
  — *Every nighte and alle,*
The fire sall never make thee shrink;
  And Christe receive thy saule.

If meat or drink thou ne'er gav'st nane,
  – *Every nighte and alle,*
The fire will burn thee to the bare bane;
  And Christe receive thy saule.

This ae nighte, this ae nighte,
  – *Every nighte and alle,*
Fire and fleet and candle-lighte,
  And Christe receive thy saule.

ANON

The Twa Corbies

As I was walking all alane,
I heard twa corbies making a mean;
The tane unto the t'other gan say,
'Whaur sall we gang and dine today?'

'In behint yon auld fail dyke,
I wot there lies a new-slain knight;
And naebody kens that he lies there,
But his hawk, his hound, and his lady fair.

'His hound is to the hunting gane,
His hawk to fetch the wildfowl hame,
His lady's ta'en another mate,
Sae we may mak' our dinner sweet.

'Ye sall sit on his white hause bane,
And I'll pyke out his bonny blue een,
Wi' ae lock o' his gowden hair,
We'll theek our nest when it grows bare.

'Mony a ane for him makes mean,
But nane sall ken whaur he is gane;
O'er his white banes when they are bare,
The wind sall blaw for evermair.'

ANON

Unwelcome

We were young, we were merry, we were very very wise,
    And the door stood open at our feast,
When there passed us a woman with the West in her eyes,
    And a man with his back to the East.

O, still grew the hearts that were beating so fast,
    The loudest voice was still.
The jest died away on our lips as they passed,
    And the rays of July struck chill.

The cups of red wine turned pale on the board,
    The white bread black as soot.
The hound forgot the hand of her lord,
    She fell down at his foot.

Low let me lie, where the dead dog lies,
    Ere I sit me down again at a feast,
When there passes a woman with the West in her eyes,
    And a man with his back to the East.

MARY COLERIDGE

The Fairies

(A Child's Song)

Up the airy mountain,
    Down the rushy glen,
We daren't go a hunting
    For fear of little men;
Wee folk, good folk,
    Trooping all together;
Green jacket, red cap,
    And white owl's feather!

Down along the rocky shore
    Some make their home,
They live on crispy pancakes
    Of yellow-tide foam;

Some in the reeds
  Of the black mountain-lake,
With frogs for their watch-dogs,
  All night awake.

High on the hill-top
  The old King sits;
He is now so old and gray
  He's nigh lost his wits.
With a bridge of white mist
  Columbkill he crosses,
On his stately journeys
  From Slieveleague to Rosses;
Or going up with music
  On cold starry nights,
To sup with the Queen
  Of the gay Northern Lights.

They stole little Bridget
  For seven years long;
When she came down again
  Her friends were all gone.
They took her lightly back,
  Between the night and morrow,
They thought that she was fast asleep,
  But she was dead with sorrow.
They have kept her ever since
  Deep within the lakes,
On a bed of flag-leaves,
  Watching till she wakes.

By the craggy hill-side,
  Through the mosses bare,
They have planted thorn-trees
  For pleasure here and there.
Is any man so daring
  As dig them up in spite,
He shall find their sharpest thorns
  In his bed at night.

Up the airy mountain,
  Down the rushy glen,
We daren't go a hunting
  For fear of little men;

Wee folk, good folk,
    Trooping all together;
Green jacket, red cap,
    And white owl's feather!

WILLIAM ALLINGHAM

'I have a young Sister'

I have a young sister
    Far beyond the sea;
Many are the keepsakes
    That she's sent me.

She sent me a cherry –
    It hadn't any stone;
And so she did a wood dove
    Withouten any bone.

She sent me a briar
    Withouten any rind;
She bade me love my sweetheart
    Withouten longing in my mind.

How should any cherry
    Be withouten stone?
And how should any wood dove
    Be withouten bone?

How should any briar,
    Be withouten rind?
And how love a sweetheart
    Withouten longing in my mind?

When the cherry was a flower
    Then it had no stone;
When the wood-dove was an egg
    Then it had no bone.

44

When the briar was unbred
  Then it had no rind;
And when a maid hath that she loves,
  She longs not in her mind.

ANON

The Splendour Falls

The splendour falls on castle walls
  And snowy summits old in story:
The long light shakes across the lakes,
  And the wild cataract leaps in glory.
Blow, bugle, blow, set the wild echoes flying,
Blow, bugle; answer, echoes, dying, dying, dying.

O hark, O hear! how thin and clear,
  And thinner, clearer, farther going!
O sweet and far from cliff and scar
  The horns of Elfland faintly blowing!
Blow, let us hear the purple glens replying:
Blow, bugle; answer, echoes, dying, dying, dying.

O love, they die in yon rich sky,
  They faint on hill or field or river:
Our echoes roll from soul to soul,
  And grow for ever and for ever.
Blow, bugle, blow, set the wild echoes flying,
And answer, echoes, answer, dying, dying, dying.

ALFRED, LORD TENNYSON

La Belle Dame Sans Merci

Oh, what can ail thee, knight-at-arms,
  Alone and palely loitering?
The sedge has withered from the lake,
  And no birds sing!

45

Oh, what can ail thee, knight-at-arms,
    So haggard and so woe-begone?
The squirrel's granary is full,
    And the harvest's done.

I see a lily on thy brow,
    With anguish moist and fever-dew,
And on thy cheek a fading rose
    Fast withereth too.

I met a lady in the meads
    Full beautiful, a fairy's child,
Her hair was long, her foot was light,
    And her eyes were wild.

I made a garland for her head,
    And bracelets too, and fragrant zone;
She looked at me as she did love,
    And made sweet moan.

I set her on my pacing steed,
    And nothing else saw all day long;
For sidelong would she bend, and sing
    A fairy's song.

She found me roots of relish sweet,
    And honey wild, and manna dew;
And sure in language strange she said,
    'I love thee true'.

She took me to her elfin grot,
    And there she wept, and sighed full sore,
And there I shut her wild wild eyes
    With kisses four.

And there she lullèd me asleep,
    And there I dreamed – Ah! woe betide! –
The latest dream I ever dreamed
    On the cold hill side.

I saw pale kings, and princes too,
    Pale warriors, death-pale were they all;
They cried – 'La belle Dame sans merci
    Hath thee in thrall!'

I saw their starved lips in the gloam
  With horrid warning gapèd wide,
And I awoke, and found me here
  On the cold hill side.

And this is why I sojourn here,
  Alone and palely loitering,
Though the sedge is withered from the lake,
  And no birds sing.

JOHN KEATS

'I saw a peacock'

I saw a peacock with a fiery tail
I saw a blazing comet drop down hail
I saw a cloud with ivy circled round
I saw a sturdy oak creep on the ground
I saw a pismire swallow up a whale
I saw a raging sea brim full of ale
I saw a Venice glass sixteen foot deep
I saw a well full of men's tears that weep
I saw their eyes all in a flame of fire
I saw a house as big as the moon and higher
I saw the sun even in the midst of night
I saw the man that saw this wondrous sight.

ANON

The Song of Wandering Aengus

I went out to the hazel wood,
Because a fire was in my head,
And cut and peeled a hazel wand,
And hooked a berry to a thread;
And when white moths were on the wing,
And moth-like stars were flickering out,
I dropped the berry in a stream
And caught a little silver trout.

When I had laid it on the floor
I went to blow the fire aflame,
But something rustled on the floor,
And some one called me by my name:
It had become a glimmering girl
With apple blossom in her hair
Who called me by my name and ran
And faded through the brightening air.

Though I am old with wandering
Through hollow lands and hilly lands,
I will find out where she has gone,
And kiss her lips and take her hands;
And walk among long dappled grass,
And pluck till time and times are done
The silver apples of the moon,
The golden apples of the sun.

W.B. YEATS

The Way through the Woods

They shut the road through the woods
Seventy years ago.
Weather and rain have undone it again,
And now you would never know
There was once a road through the woods
Before they planted the trees.
It is underneath the coppice and heath
And the thin anemones.
Only the keeper sees
That, where the ring-dove broods,
And the badgers roll at ease,
There was once a road through the woods.

Yet, if you enter the woods
Of a summer evening late,
When the night-air cools on the trout-ringed pools
Where the otter whistles his mate,
(They fear not men in the woods,
Because they see so few.)

You will hear the beat of a horse's feet,
And the swish of a skirt in the dew,
Steadily cantering through
The misty solitudes,
As though they perfectly knew
The old lost road through the woods. . . .
But there is no road through the woods.

RUDYARD KIPLING

Tom o' Bedlam

The moon's my constant mistress,
    And the lovely owl my marrow;
        The flaming drake,
        And the night-crow, make
    Me music to my sorrow.

I know more than Apollo;
    For oft, when he lies sleeping,
        I behold the stars
        At mortal wars,
    And the rounded welkin weeping.

The moon embraces her shepherd,
    And the Queen of Love her warrior
        While the first does horn
        The stars of the morn,
    And the next the heavenly farrier.

With a heart of furious fancies,
    Whereof I am commander:
        With a burning spear,
        And a horse of air,
    To the wilderness I wander;

With a Knight of ghosts and shadows,
    I summoned am to Tourney:
        Ten leagues beyond
        The wide world's end;
    Methinks it is no journey.

ANON

Kubla Khan

In Xanadu did Kubla Khan
A stately pleasure-dome decree:
Where Alph, the sacred river, ran
Through caverns measureless to man
  Down to a sunless sea.
So twice five miles of fertile ground
With walls and towers were girdled round:
And there were gardens bright with sinuous rills
Where blossomed many an incense-bearing tree;
And here were forests ancient as the hills,
Enfolding sunny spots of greenery.

But oh! that deep romantic chasm which slanted
Down the green hill athwart a cedarn cover!
A savage place! as holy and enchanted
As e'er beneath a waning moon was haunted
By woman wailing for her demon-lover!
And from this chasm, with ceaseless turmoil seething,
As if this earth in fast thick pants were breathing,
A mighty fountain momently was forced:
Amid whose swift half-intermitted burst
Huge fragments vaulted like rebounding hail,
Or chaffy grain beneath the thresher's flail:
And mid these dancing rocks at once and ever
It flung up momently the sacred river.
Five miles meandering with a mazy motion
Through wood and dale the sacred river ran,
Then reached the caverns measureless to man,
And sank in tumult to a lifeless ocean:
And 'mid this tumult Kubla heard from far
Ancestral voices prophesying war!

  The shadow of the dome of pleasure
  Floated midway on the waves;
  Where was heard the mingled measure
  From the fountain and the caves.
It was a miracle of rare device,
A sunny pleasure-dome with caves of ice!

  A damsel with a dulcimer
  In a vision once I saw:
  It was an Abyssinian maid,

And on her dulcimer she played,
Singing of Mount Abora.
Could I revive within me
Her symphony and song,
To such a deep delight 'twould win me
That with music loud and long,
I would build that dome in air,
That sunny dome! those caves of ice!
And all who heard should see them there,
And all should cry, Beware! Beware!
His flashing eyes, his floating hair!
Weave a circle round him thrice,
And close your eyes with holy dread,
For he on honey-dew hath fed,
And drunk the milk of Paradise.

SAMUEL TAYLOR COLERIDGE

Jabberwocky

'Twas brillig, and the slithy toves
　Did gyre and gimble in the wabe:
All mimsy were the borogoves,
　　And the mome raths outgrabe.

'Beware the Jabberwock, my son!
　The jaws that bite, the claws that catch!
Beware the Jubjub bird, and shun
　　The frumious Bandersnatch!'

He took his vorpal sword in hand:
　Long time the manxome foe he sought –
So rested he by the Tumtum tree,
　　And stood awhile in thought.

And, as in uffish thought he stood,
　The Jabberwock, with eyes of flame,
Came whiffling through the tulgey wood,
　　And burbled as it came!

One, two! One, two! And through and through
    The vorpal blade went snicker-snack!
He left it dead, and with its head
    He went galumphing back.

'And hast thou slain the Jabberwock?
    Come to my arms, my beamish boy!
O frabjous day! Callooh! Callay!'
    He chortled in his joy.

'Twas brillig, and the slithy toves
    Did gyre and gimble in the wabe:
All mimsy were the borogoves,
    And the mome raths outgrabe.

LEWIS CARROLL

The Call

From our low seat beside the fire
    Where we have dozed and dreamed and watched the glow
Or raked the ashes, stopping so
We scarcely saw the sun or rain
    Above, or looked much higher
Than this same quiet red or burned-out fire.
        To-night we heard a call,
        A rattle on the window-pane,
        A voice on the sharp air,
And felt a breath stirring our hair,
    A flame within us: Something swift and tall
Swept in and out and that was all.
Was it a bright or a dark angel? Who can know?
    It left no mark upon the snow,
        But suddenly it snapped the chain
        Unbarred, flung wide the door
        Which will not shut again;
And so we cannot sit here any more.
        We must arise and go:
        The world is cold without
        And dark and hedged about

With mystery and enmity and doubt,
　　But we must go
　　Though yet we do not know
Who called, or what marks we shall leave upon the snow.

CHARLOTTE MEW

The Listeners

'Is there anybody there?' said the Traveller,
　　Knocking on the moonlit door;
And his horse in the silence champed the grasses
　　Of the forest's ferny floor:
And a bird flew up out of the turret,
　　Above the Traveller's head:
And he smote upon the door again a second time;
　　'Is there anybody there?' he said.
But no one descended to the Traveller;
　　No head from the leaf-fringed sill
Leaned over and looked into his grey eyes,
　　Where he stood perplexed and still.
But only a host of phantom listeners
　　That dwelt in the lone house then
Stood listening in the quiet of the moonlight
　　To that voice from the world of men:
Stood thronging the faint moonbeams on the dark stair,
　　That goes down to the empty hall,
Hearkening in an air stirred and shaken
　　By the lonely Traveller's call.
And he felt in his heart their strangeness,
　　Their stillness answering his cry,
While his horse moved, cropping the dark turf,
　　'Neath the starred and leafy sky;
For he suddenly smote on the door, even
　　Louder, and lifted his head: –
'Tell them I came, and no one answered,
　　That I kept my word,' he said.
Never the least stir made the listeners,
　　Though every word he spake
Fell echoing through the shadowiness of the still house
　　From the one man left awake:

Ay, they heard his foot upon the stirrup,
  And the sound of iron on stone,
And how the silence surged softly backward,
  When the plunging hoofs were gone.

WALTER DE LA MARE

'There are men in the village of Erith'

There are men in the village of Erith
    Whom nobody seeth or heareth,
    And there looms, on the marge
    Of the river, a barge
That nobody roweth or steereth.

ANON

'Hark, hark, the dogs do bark'

Hark, hark, the dogs do bark,
  The beggars are coming to town;
Some in rags, and some in jags,
  And one in a velvet gown.

ANON

The cauld Lad of Hilton

Wae's me! wae's me!
The acorn's not yet
Fallen from the tree
That's to grow the wood,
That's to make the cradle,
That's to rock the bairn,
That's to grow to a man,
That's to lay me.

ANON

The Raven

Once upon a midnight dreary, while I pondered, weak and weary,
Over many a quaint and curious volume of forgotten lore –
While I nodded, nearly napping, suddenly there came a tapping,
As of some one gently rapping, rapping at my chamber door.
"'T is some visiter," I muttered, "tapping at my chamber door –
                            Only this and nothing more."

Ah, distinctly I remember it was in the bleak December;
And each separate dying ember wrought its ghost upon the floor.
Eagerly I wished the morrow; – vainly I had sought to borrow
From my books surcease of sorrow – sorrow for the lost Lenore –
For the rare and radiant maiden whom the angels name Lenore –
                            Nameless *here* for evermore.

And the silken, sad, uncertain rustling of each purple curtain
Thrilled me – filled me with fantastic terrors never felt before;
So that now, to still the beating of my heart, I stood repeating
"'T is some visiter entreating entrance at my chamber door –
Some late visiter entreating entrance at my chamber door; –
                            This it is and nothing more."

Presently my soul grew stronger; hesitating then no longer,
"Sir," said I, "or Madam, truly your forgiveness I implore;
But the fact is I was napping, and so gently you came rapping,
And so faintly you came tapping, tapping at my chamber door,
That I scarce was sure I heard you" – here I opened wide the door; –
                            Darkness there and nothing more.

Deep into that darkness peering, long I stood there wondering,
     fearing,
Doubting, dreaming dreams no mortal ever dared to dream before;
But the silence was unbroken, and the stillness gave no token,
And the only word there spoken was the whispered word, "Lenore!"
This I whispered, and an echo murmured back the word "Lenore!"
                            Merely this and nothing more.

Back into the chamber turning, all my soul within me burning,
Soon again I heard a tapping somewhat louder than before.
"Surely," said I, "surely that is something at my window lattice;
Let me see, then, what thereat is, and this mystery explore –
Let my heart be still a moment and this mystery explore; –
                            'T is the wind and nothing more!"

Open here I flung the shutter, when, with many a flirt and flutter
In there stepped a stately Raven of the saintly days of yore.
Not the least obeisance made he; not a minute stopped or stayed he;
But, with mien of lord or lady, perched above my chamber door –
Perched upon a bust of Pallas just above my chamber door –
                    Perched, and sat, and nothing more.

Then this ebony bird beguiling my sad fancy into smiling,
By the grave and stern decorum of the countenance it wore,
"Though thy crest be shorn and shaven, thou," I said, "art sure
    no craven,
Ghastly grim and ancient Raven wandering from the Nightly
    shore –
Tell me what thy lordly name is on the Night's Plutonian shore!"
                    Quoth the Raven, "Nevermore."

Much I marvelled this ungainly fowl to hear discourse so plainly,
Though its answer little meaning – little relevancy bore;
For we cannot help agreeing that no living human being
Ever yet was blessed with seeing bird above his chamber door –
Bird or beast upon the sculptured bust above his chamber door,
                    With such name as "Nevermore."

But the Raven, sitting lonely on the placid bust, spoke only
That one word, as if his soul in that one word he did outpour.
Nothing farther then he uttered – not a feather then he fluttered –
Till I scarcely more than muttered "Other friends have flown before.
On the morrow *he* will leave me, as my hopes have flown before."
                    Then the bird said "Nevermore."

Startled at the stillness broken by reply so aptly spoken,
"Doubtless," said I, "what it utters is its only stock and store
Caught from some unhappy master whom unmerciful Disaster
Followed fast and followed faster till his songs one burden bore –
Till the dirges of his Hope that melancholy burden bore
                    Of 'Never – nevermore.'"

But the Raven still beguiling all my fancy into smiling,
Straight I wheeled a cushioned seat in front of bird, and bust and
    door;
Then, upon the velvet sinking, I betook myself to linking
Fancy unto fancy, thinking what this ominous bird of yore –
What this grim, ungainly, ghastly, gaunt, and ominous bird of yore
                    Meant in croaking "Nevermore."

This I sat engaged in guessing, but no syllable expressing
To the fowl whose fiery eyes now burned into my bosom's core;
This and more I sat divining, with my head at ease reclining
On the cushion's velvet lining that the lamp-light gloated o'er,
But whose velvet violet lining with the lamp-light gloating o'er,
                              She shall press, ah, nevermore!

Then, methought, the air grew denser, perfumed from an unseen
    censer
Swung by Seraphim whose foot-falls tinkled on the tufted floor.
"Wretch," I cried, "thy God hath lent thee – by these angels he
    hath sent thee
Respite – respite and nepenthe from thy memories of Lenore;
Quaff, oh quaff this kind nepenthe and forget this lost Lenore!"
                              Quoth the Raven "Nevermore."

"Prophet!" said I, "thing of evil! prophet still, if bird or devil! –
Whether Tempter sent, or whether tempest tossed thee here
    ashore,
Desolate yet all undaunted, on this desert land enchanted –
On this home by Horror haunted – tell me truly, I implore –
Is there – *is* there balm in Gilead? – tell me – tell me, I implore!"
                              Quoth the Raven "Nevermore."

"Prophet!" said I, "thing of evil! – prophet still, if bird or devil!
By that Heaven that bends above us – by that God we both
    adore –
Tell this soul with sorrow laden if, within the distant Aidenn,
It shall clasp a sainted maiden whom the angels name Lenore –
Clasp a rare and radiant maiden whom the angels name Lenore."
                              Quoth the Raven "Nevermore."

"Be that word our sign of parting, bird or fiend!" I shrieked,
    upstarting –
"Get thee back into the tempest and the Night's Plutonian shore!
Leave no black plume as a token of that lie thy soul hath spoken!
Leave my loneliness unbroken! – quit the bust above my door!
Take thy beak from out my heart, and take thy form from off my
    door!"
                              Quoth the Raven "Nevermore."

And the Raven, never flitting, still is sitting, *still* is sitting
On the pallid bust of Pallas just above my chamber door;
And his eyes have all the seeming of a demon's that is dreaming,

And the lamp-light o'er him streaming throws his shadow on the
    floor;
And my soul from out that shadow that lies floating on the floor
                    Shall be lifted – nevermore!

EDGAR ALLAN POE

The Witch's Ballad

O, I hae come from far away,
  From a warm land far away,
A southern land across the sea,
With sailor-lads about the mast,
Merry and canny, and kind to me.

And I hae been to yon town
  To try my luck in yon town;
Nort, and Mysie, Elspie too.
Right braw we were to pass the gate,
Wi' gowden clasps on girdles blue.

Mysie smiled wi' miminy mouth,
  Innocent mouth, miminy mouth;
Elspie wore a scarlet gown,
Nort's grey eyes were unco' gleg,
My Castile comb was like a crown.

We walk'd abreast all up the street,
  Into the market up the street;
Our hair with marigolds was wound,
Our bodices with love-knots laced,
Our merchandise with tansy bound.

Nort had chickens, I had cocks,
  Gamesome cocks, loud-crowing cocks;
Mysie ducks, and Elspie drakes, –
For a wee groat or a pound;
We lost nae time wi' gives and takes.

58

Lost nae time, for well we knew,
  In our sleeves full well we knew,
When the gloaming came that night,
Duck nor drake, nor hen nor cock
Would be found by candle-light.

And when our chaffering all was done,
  All was paid for, sold and done,
We drew a glove on ilka hand,
We sweetly curtsied, each to each,
And deftly danced a saraband.

The market-lassies look'd and laugh'd,
  Left their gear, and look'd and laugh'd;
They made as they would join the game,
But soon their mithers, wild and wud,
With whack and screech they stopp'd the same.

Sae loud the tongues o' randies grew,
  The flytin' and the skirlin' grew,
At all the windows in the place,
Wi' spoons or knives, wi' needle or awl,
Was thrust out every hand and face.

And down each stair they throng'd anon,
  Gentle, semple, throng'd anon;
Souter and tailor, frowsy Nan,
The ancient widow young again,
Simpering behind her fan.

Without a choice, against their will,
  Doited, dazed, against their will,
The market lassie and her mither,
The farmer and his husbandman,
Hand in hand dance a' thegither.

Slow at first, but faster soon,
  Still increasing, wild and fast,
Hoods and mantles, hats and hose,
Blindly doff'd and cast away,
Left them naked, heads and toes.

They would have torn us limb from limb,
    Dainty limb from dainty limb;
But never one of them could win
Across the line that I had drawn
With bleeding thumb a-widdershin.

But there was Jeff the provost's son,
    Jeff the provost's only son;
There was Father Auld himsel',
The Lombard frae the hostelry,
And the lawyer Peter Fell.

All goodly men we singled out,
    Waled them well, and singled out,
And drew them by the left hand in;
Mysie the priest, and Elspie won
The Lombard, Nort the lawyer carle,
I mysel' the provost's son.

Then, with cantrip kisses seven,
    Three times round with kisses seven,
Warp'd and woven there spun we
Arms and legs and flaming hair,
Like a whirlwind on the sea.

Like a wind that sucks the sea,
    Over and in and on the sea,
Good sooth it was a mad delight;
And every man of all the four
Shut his eyes and laugh'd outright.

Laugh'd as long as they had breath,
    Laugh'd while they had sense or breath;
And close about us coil'd a mist
Of gnats and midges, wasps and flies,
Like the whirlwind shaft it rist.

Drawn up I was right off my feet,
    Into the mist and off my feet;
And, dancing on each chimney-top,
I saw a thousand darling imps
Keeping time with skip and hop.

And on the provost's brave ridge-tile,
   On the provost's grand ridge-tile,
The Blackamoor first to master me
I saw, I saw that winsome smile,
The mouth that did my heart beguile,
And spoke the great Word over me,
In the land beyond the sea.

I call'd his name, I call'd aloud,
   Alas! I call'd on him aloud;
And then he fill'd his hand with stour,
And threw it towards me in the air;
My mouse flew out, I lost my pow'r!

My lusty strength, my power were gone;
   Power was gone, and all was gone.
He will not let me love him more!
Of bell and whip and horse's tail
He cares not if I find a store.

But I am proud if he is fierce!
   I am as proud as he is fierce;
I'll turn about and backward go,
If I meet again that Blackamoor,
And he'll help us then, for he shall know
I seek another paramour.

And we'll gang once more to yon town,
   Wi' better luck to yon town;
We'll walk in silk and cramoisie,
And I shall wed the provost's son,
My lady of the town I'll be!

For I was born a crown'd king's child,
   Born and nursed a king's child,
King o' a land ayont the sea,
Where the Blackamoor kiss'd me first,
And taught me art and glamourie.

Each one in her wame shall hide
   Her hairy mouse, her wary mouse,
Fed on madwort, and agramie, –
Wear amber beads between her breasts,
And blind-worm's skin about her knee.

The Lombard shall be Elspie's man,
    Elspie's gowden husband-man;
Nort shall take the lawyer's hand;
The priest shall swear another vow:
We'll dance again the saraband!

WILLIAM BELL SCOTT

Tony O!

Over the bleak and barren snow
A voice there came a-calling;
"Where are you going to, Tony O!
Where are you going this morning?"

"I am going where there are rivers of wine,
The mountains bread and honey;
There Kings and Queens do mind the swine,
And the poor have all the money."

COLIN FRANCIS

Lost Love

His eyes are quickened so with grief,
He can watch a grass or leaf
Every instant grow; he can
Clearly through a flint wall see,
Or watch the startled spirit flee
From the throat of a dead man.
    Across two counties he can hear
And catch your words before you speak.
The woodlouse or the maggot's weak
Clamour rings in his sad ear,
And noise so slight it would surpass
Credence – drinking sound of grass,
Worm talk, clashing jaws of moth
Chumbling holes in cloth;

62

The groan of ants who undertake
Gigantic loads for honour's sake
(Their sinews creak, their breath comes thin);
Whir of spiders when they spin,
And minute whispering, mumbling, sighs
Of idle grubs and flies.
 This man is quickened so with grief,
He wanders god-like or like thief
Inside and out, below, above,
Without relief seeking lost love.

ROBERT GRAVES

'There was a man of double deed'

There was a man of double deed
Who sowed his garden full of seed;
And when the seed began to grow,
'Twas like a garden full of snow;
And when the snow began to fall,
Like birds it was upon the wall;
And when the birds began to fly,
'Twas like a shipwreck in the sky;
And when the sky began to crack,
'Twas like a stick upon my back;
And when my back began to smart,
'Twas like a pen-knife in my heart;
And when my heart began to bleed,
Then I was dead – and dead indeed.

ANON

Epilogue from The Orators

'O where are you going?' said reader to rider,
'That valley is fatal where furnaces burn,
Yonder's the midden whose odours will madden,
That gap is the grave where the tall return.'

'O do you imagine', said fearer to farer,
'That dusk will delay on your path to the pass,
Your diligent looking discover the lacking
Your footsteps feel from granite to grass?'

'O what was that bird', said horror to hearer,
'Did you see that shape in the twisted trees?
Behind you swiftly the figure comes softly,
The spot on your skin is a shocking disease?'

'Out of this house' – said rider to reader
'Yours never will' – said farer to fearer
'They're looking for you' – said hearer to horror
As he left them there, as he left them there.

W.H. AUDEN

The Mother's Son

I have a dream – a dreadful dream –
  A dream that is never done,
I watch a man go out of his mind,
  And he is My Mother's Son.

They pushed him into a Mental Home,
  And that is like the grave:
For they do not let you sleep upstairs,
  And you're not allowed to shave.

And it was *not* disease or crime
  Which got him landed there,
But because They laid on My Mother's Son
  More than a man could bear.

What with noise, and fear of death,
  Waking, and wounds and cold,
They filled the Cup for My Mother's Son
  Fuller than it could hold.

64

They broke his body and his mind
   And yet They made him live,
And They asked more of My Mother's Son
   Than any man could give.

For, just because he had not died
   Nor been discharged nor sick:
They dragged it out with My Mother's Son
   Longer than he could stick....

And no one knows when he'll get well –
   So, there he'll have to be:
And, 'spite of the beard in the looking-glass,
   I know that man is me!

                    RUDYARD KIPLING

My Last Duchess

Ferrara

That's my last Duchess painted on the wall,
Looking as if she were alive. I call
That piece a wonder, now: Frà Pandolf's hands
Worked busily a day, and there she stands.
Will 't please you sit and look at her? I said
"Frà Pandolf" by design, for never read
Strangers like you that pictured countenance,
The depth and passion of its earnest glance,
But to myself they turned (since none puts by
The curtain I have drawn for you, but I)
And seemed as they would ask me, if they durst,
How such a glance came there; so, not the first
Are you to turn and ask thus. Sir, 't was not
Her husband's presence only, called that spot
Of joy into the Duchess' cheek: perhaps
Frà Pandolf chanced to say "Her mantle laps
"Over my lady's wrist too much," or "Paint
"Must never hope to reproduce the faint
"Half-flush that dies along her throat:" such stuff
Was courtesy, she thought, and cause enough
For calling up that spot of joy. She had

A heart – how shall I say? – too soon made glad,
Too easily impressed; she liked whate'er
She looked on, and her looks went everywhere.
Sir, 't was all one! My favour at her breast,
The dropping of the daylight in the West,
The bough of cherries some officious fool
Broke in the orchard for her, the white mule
She rode with round the terrace – all and each
Would draw from her alike the approving speech,
Or blush, at least. She thanked men, – good! but thanked
Somehow – I know not how – as if she ranked
My gift of a nine-hundred-years-old name
With anybody's gift. Who'd stoop to blame
This sort of trifling? Even had you skill
In speech – (which I have not) – to make your will
Quite clear to such an one, and say, "Just this
"Or that in you disgusts me; here you miss,
"Or there exceed the mark" – and if she let
Herself be lessoned so, nor plainly set
Her wits to yours, forsooth, and made excuse,
– E'en then would be some stooping and I choose
Never to stoop. Oh sir, she smiled, no doubt,
Whene'er I passed her; but who passed without
Much the same smile? This grew; I gave commands;
Then all smiles stopped together. There she stands
As if alive. Will 't please you rise? We'll meet
The company below, then. I repeat,
The Count your master's known munificence
Is ample warrant that no just pretence
Of mine for dowry will be disallowed;
Though his fair daughter's self, as I avowed
At starting, is my object. Nay, we'll go
Together down, sir. Notice Neptune, though,
Taming a sea-horse, thought a rarity,
Which Claus of Innsbruck cast in bronze for me!

ROBERT BROWNING

Beliefs and Doubts

'Love bade me welcome'

Love bade me welcome: yet my soul drew back,
      Guilty of dust and sin.
But quick-eyed Love, observing me grow slack
      From my first entrance in,
Drew nearer to me, sweetly questioning,
      If I lacked any thing.

A guest, I answered, worthy to be here:
      Love said, You shall be he.
I the unkind, ungrateful? Ah my dear,
      I cannot look on thee.
Love took my hand, and smiling did reply,
      Who made the eyes but I?

Truth Lord, but I have marred them: let my shame
      Go where it doth deserve.
And know you not, says Love, who bore the blame?
      My dear, then I will serve.
You must sit down, says Love, and taste my meat:
      So I did sit and eat.

GEORGE HERBERT

My Master hath a Garden

My master hath a garden, full-filled with divers flowers,
Where thou may'st gather posies gay, all times and hours,
      Here nought is heard
      But paradise-bird,
      Harp, dulcimer, and lute,
        With cymbal,
        And timbrel,
      And the gentle sounding flute.

Oh! Jesus, Lord, my heal and weal, my bliss complete,
Make thou my heart thy garden-plot, true, fair and neat
                    That I may hear
                    This music clear,
                    Harp, dulcimer, and lute,
                        With cymbal,
                        And timbrel,
                    And the gentle sounding flute.

ANON

Another Grace for a Child

Here a little child I stand,
Heaving up my either hand;
Cold as Paddocks though they be,
Here I lift them up to Thee,
For a Benizon to fall
On our meat, and on us all. *Amen.*

ROBERT HERRICK

Up-hill

Does the road wind up-hill all the way?
    Yes, to the very end.
Will the day's journey take the whole long day?
    From morn to night, my friend.

But is there for the night a resting-place?
    A roof for when the slow dark hours begin.
May not the darkness hide it from my face?
    You cannot miss that inn.

Shall I meet other wayfarers at night?
    Those who have gone before.
Then must I knock, or call when just in sight?
    They will not keep you standing at that door.

Shall I find comfort, travel-sore and weak?
  Of labour you shall find the sum.
Will there be beds for me and all who seek?
  Yea, beds for all who come.

CHRISTINA ROSSETTI

'The man of life upright'

The man of life upright,
  Whose cheerful mind is free
From weight of impious deeds
  And yoke of vanity;

The man whose silent days
  In harmless joys are spent:
Whom hopes cannot delude,
  Nor sorrows discontent;

That man needs neither towers,
  Nor armour for defence:
Nor vaults his guilt to shroud
  From thunder's violence;

He only can behold
  With unaffrighted eyes
The horrors of the deep,
  And terrors of the Skies.

Thus, scorning all the cares
  That fate or fortune brings,
His Book the Heav'ns he makes,
  His wisdom heav'nly things;

Good thoughts his surest friends,
  His wealth a well-spent age,
The earth his sober Inn,
  And quiet pilgrimage.

THOMAS CAMPION

Magna Est Veritas

Here, in this little Bay,
Full of tumultuous life and great repose,
Where, twice a day,
The purposeless, glad ocean comes and goes,
Under high cliffs, and far from the huge town,
I sit me down.
For want of me the world's course will not fail:
When all its work is done, the lie shall rot;
The truth is great, and shall prevail,
When none cares whether it prevail or not.

COVENTRY PATMORE

Mimnermus in Church

You promise heavens free from strife,
    Pure truth, and perfect change of will;
But sweet, sweet is this human life,
    So sweet, I fain would breathe it still;
Your chilly stars I can forgo,
This warm kind world is all I know.

You say there is no substance here,
    One great reality above:
Back from that void I shrink in fear,
    And child-like hide myself in love:
Show me what angels feel. Till then,
I cling, a mere weak man, to men.

You bid me lift my mean desires
    From faltering lips and fitful veins
To sexless souls, ideal quires,
    Unwearied voices, wordless strains:
My mind with fonder welcome owns
One dear dead friend's remembered tones.

70

Forsooth the present we must give
    To that which cannot pass away;
All beauteous things for which we live
    By laws of time and space decay.
But oh, the very reason why
I clasp them, is because they die.

WILLIAM CORY

Prayer

Prayer the Church's banquet, Angels' age,
    Gods breath in man returning to his birth,
    The soul in paraphrase, heart in pilgrimage,
The Christian plummet sounding heav'n and earth;
Engine against th' Almighty, sinners' tower,
    Reversed thunder, Christ-side-piercing spear,
    The six-days' world transposing in an hour,
A kind of tune, which all things hear and fear;
Softness, and peace, and joy, and love, and bliss,
    Exalted Manna, gladness of the best,
    Heaven in ordinary, man well drest,
The milky way, the bird of Paradise,
    Church-bells beyond the stars heard, the soul's blood,
    The land of spices; something understood.

GEORGE HERBERT

'"Faith" is a fine invention'

"Faith" is a fine invention
When Gentlemen can *see* –
But *Microscopes* are prudent
In an Emergency.

EMILY DICKINSON

71

A Royal Guest

... Yet if His Majesty our sovereign lord
    Should of his own accord
    Friendly himself invite,
And say, "I'll be your guest to-morrow night,"
How should we stir ourselves, call and command
All hands to work! "Let no man idle stand!

"Set me fine Spanish tables in the hall,
    See they be fitted all;
    Let there be room to eat,
And order taken that there want no meat.
See every sconce and candlestick made bright,
That without tapers they may give a light.

"Look to the presence: are the carpets spread,
    The dazie o'er the head,
    The cushions in the chairs,
And all the candles lighted on the stairs?
Perfume the chambers, and in any case
Let each man give attendance in his place!"

Thus, if the king were coming, would we do,
    And 't were good reason too;
    For 'tis a duteous thing
To show all honour to an earthly king,
And after all our travail and our cost,
So he be pleased, to think no labour lost.

But at the coming of the King of Heaven
    All's set at six and seven:
    We wallow in our sin,
Christ cannot find a chamber in the inn.
We entertain Him always like a stranger,
And, as at first, still lodge Him in a manger.

ANON

Dover Beach

The sea is calm tonight.
The tide lies full, the moon lies fair
Upon the straits; – on the French coast the light
Gleams and is gone; the cliffs of England stand,
Glimmering and vast, out in the tranquil bay.
Come to the window, sweet is the night-air!
Only, from the long line of spray
Where the sea meets the moon-blanch'd land,
Listen! you hear the grating roar
Of pebbles which the waves draw back, and fling,
At their return, up the high strand,
Begin, and cease, and then again begin,
With tremulous cadence slow, and bring
The eternal note of sadness in.

Sophocles long ago
Heard it on the Ægæan, and it brought
Into his mind the turbid ebb and flow
Of human misery; we
Find also in the sound a thought,
Hearing it by this distant northern sea.

The Sea of Faith
Was once, too, at the full, and round earth's shore
Lay like the folds of a bright girdle furl'd.
But now I only hear
Its melancholy, long, withdrawing roar,
Retreating, to the breath
Of the night-wind, down the vast edges drear
And naked shingles of the world.

Ah, love, let us be true
To one another! for the world, which seems
To lie before us like a land of dreams,
So various, so beautiful, so new,
Hath really neither joy, nor love, nor light,
Nor certitude, nor peace, nor help for pain;
And we are here as on a darkling plain
Swept with confused alarms of struggle and flight,
Where ignorant armies clash by night.

MATTHEW ARNOLD

The Dark Angel

Dark Angel, with thine aching lust
To rid the world of penitence:
Malicious Angel, who still dost
My soul such subtile violence!

Because of thee, no thought, no thing,
Abides for me undesecrate:
Dark Angel, ever on the wing,
Who never reachest me too late!

When music sounds, then changest thou
Its silvery to a sultry fire:
Nor will thine envious heart allow
Delight untortured by desire.

Through thee, the gracious Muses turn
To Furies, O mine Enemy!
And all the things of beauty burn
With flames of evil ecstasy.

Because of thee, the land of dreams
Becomes a gathering place of fears:
Until tormented slumber seems
One vehemence of useless tears.

When sunlight glows upon the flowers,
Or ripples down the dancing sea:
Thou, with thy troop of passionate powers,
Beleaguerest, bewilderest, me.

Within the breath of autumn woods,
Within the winter silences:
Thy venomous spirit stirs and broods,
O Master of impieties!

The ardour of red flame is thine,
And thine the steely soul of ice:
Thou poisonest the fair design
Of nature, with unfair device.

Apples of ashes, golden bright;
Waters of bitterness, how sweet!

O banquet of a foul delight,
Prepared by thee, dark Paraclete!

Thou art the whisper in the gloom,
The hinting tone, the haunting laugh:
Thou art the adorner of my tomb,
The minstrel of mine epitaph.

I fight thee, in the Holy Name!
Yet, what thou dost, is what God saith:
Tempter! should I escape thy flame,
Thou wilt have helped my soul from Death:

The second Death, that never dies,
That cannot die, when time is dead:
Live Death, wherein the lost soul cries,
Eternally uncomforted.

Dark Angel, with thine aching lust!
Of two defeats, of two despairs:
Less dread, a change to drifting dust,
Than thine eternity of cares.

Do what thou wilt, thou shalt not so,
Dark Angel! triumph over me:
Lonely, unto the Lone I go;
Divine, to the Divinity.

LIONEL JOHNSON

'Matthew, Mark, Luke and John'

Matthew, Mark, Luke and John,
Bless the bed that I lie on.
   Four corners to my bed,
   Four angels round my head;
   One to watch and one to pray
   And two to bear my soul away.

ANON

'Now I lay me down to sleep'

Now I lay me down to sleep;
I pray the Lord my soul to keep.
If I should die before I wake,
I pray the Lord my soul to take.

ANON

The Divine Image

To Mercy, Pity, Peace, and Love
All pray in their distress;
And to these virtues of delight
Return their thankfulness.

For Mercy, Pity, Peace, and Love
Is God, our father dear,
And Mercy, Pity, Peace, and Love
Is Man, his child and care.

For Mercy has a human heart,
Pity a human face,
And Love, the human form divine,
And Peace, the human dress.

Then every man, of every clime,
That prays in his distress,
Prays to the human form divine,
Love, Mercy, Pity, Peace.

And all must love the human form,
In heathen, Turk, or Jew;
Where Mercy, Love, & Pity dwell
There God is dwelling too.

WILLIAM BLAKE

Moralities

The Last Word

Creep into thy narrow bed,
Creep, and let no more be said!
Vain thy onset! all stands fast.
Thou thyself must break at last.

Let the long contention cease!
Geese are swans, and swans are geese.
Let them have it how they will!
Thou art tired; best be still.

They out-talk'd thee, hiss'd thee, tore thee?
Better men fared thus before thee;
Fired their ringing shot and pass'd,
Hotly charged – and sank at last.

Charge once more, then, and be dumb!
Let the victors, when they come,
When the forts of folly fall,
Find thy body by the wall!

MATTHEW ARNOLD

'Say not, the struggle nought availeth'

Say not, the struggle nought availeth,
    The labour and the wounds are vain,
The enemy faints not, nor faileth,
    And as things have been they remain.

If hopes were dupes, fears may be liars;
    It may be, in yon smoke concealed,
Your comrades chase e'en now the fliers,
    And, but for you, possess the field.

For while the tired waves, vainly breaking,
   Seem here no painful inch to gain,
Far back, through creeks and inlets making,
   Comes silent, flooding in, the main,

And not by eastern windows only,
   When daylight comes, comes in the light,
In front, the sun climbs slow, how slowly,
   But westward, look, the land is bright.

ARTHUR HUGH CLOUGH

Silence

My father used to say,
'Superior people never make long visits,
have to be shown Longfellow's grave
or the glass flowers at Harvard.
Self-reliant like the cat –
that takes its prey to privacy,
the mouse's limp tail hanging like a shoelace from its mouth –
they sometimes enjoy solitude,
and can be robbed of speech
by speech which has delighted them.
The deepest feeling always shows itself in silence;
not in silence, but restraint'.
Nor was he insincere in saying, 'Make my house your inn'.
Inns are not residences.

MARIANNE MOORE

The Galloping Cat

Oh I am a cat that likes to
Gallop about doing good
So
One day when I was
Galloping about doing good, I saw
A Figure in the path; I said:

78

Get off! (Be-
cause
I am a cat that likes to
Gallop about doing good)
But he did not move, instead
He raised his hand as if
To land me a cuff
So I made to dodge so as to
Prevent him bring it orf,
Un-for-tune-ately I slid
On a banana skin
Some Ass had left instead
Of putting in the bin. So
His hand caught me on the cheek
I tried
To lay his arm open from wrist to elbow
With my sharp teeth
Because I am
A cat that likes to gallop about doing good.
Would you believe it?
He wasn't there
My teeth met nothing but air,
But a Voice said: Poor cat,
(Meaning me) and a soft stroke
Came on me head
Since when
I have been bald.
I regard myself as
A martyr to doing good.
Also I heard a swoosh
As of wings, and saw
A halo shining at the height of
Mrs Gubbins's backyard fence,
So I thought: What's the good
Of galloping about doing good
When angels stand in the path
And do not do as they should
Such as having an arm to be bitten off
All the same I
Intend to go on being
A cat that likes to
Gallop about doing good
So
Now with my bald head I go,

Chopping the untidy flowers down, to and fro,
An' scooping up the grass to show
Underneath
The cinder path of wrath
Ha ha ha ha, ho,
Angels aren't the only ones who do not know
What's what and that
Galloping about doing good
Is a full-time job
That needs
An experienced eye of earthly
Sharpness, worth I dare say
(If you'll forgive a personal note)
A good deal more
Than all that skyey stuff
Of angels that make so bold as
To pity a cat like me that
Gallops about doing good.

STEVIE SMITH

'When lovely woman stoops to folly'

When lovely woman stoops to folly,
   And finds too late that men betray,
What charm can sooth her melancholy,
   What art can wash her guilt away?

The only art her guilt to cover,
   To hide her shame from every eye,
To give repentance to her lover,
   And wring his bosom – is to die.

OLIVER GOLDSMITH

Invictus

Out of the night that covers me,
  Black as the pit from pole to pole,
I thank whatever gods may be
  For my unconquerable soul.

In the fell clutch of circumstance
  I have not winced nor cried aloud.
Under the bludgeonings of chance
  My head is bloody, but unbowed.

Beyond this place of wrath and tears
  Looms but the Horror of the shade,
And yet the menace of the years
  Finds, and shall find, me unafraid.

It matters not how strait the gate,
  How charged with punishments the scroll,
I am the master of my fate:
  I am the captain of my soul.

W.E. HENLEY

Play up! Play up!

There's a breathless hush in the Close tonight –
  Ten to make and the match to win –
A bumping pitch and a blinding light,
  An hour to play and the last man in.
And it's not for the sake of a ribboned coat,
  Or the selfish hope of a season's fame,
But his Captain's hand on his shoulder smote –
  'Play up! play up! and play the game!'

The sand of the desert is sodden red, –
  Red with the wreck of a square that broke; –
The gatling's jammed and the Colonel dead,
  And the regiment blind with dust and smoke.
The river of death has brimmed his banks,
  And England's far, and Honour a name,

But the voice of a schoolboy rallies the ranks:
   'Play up! play up! and play the game!'

This is the word that year by year,
   While in her place the School is set,
Every one of her sons must hear,
   And none that hears it dare forget.
This they all with a joyful mind
   Bear through life like a torch in flame,
And falling fling to the host behind –
   'Play up! play up! and play the game!'

SIR HENRY NEWBOLT

If –

If you can keep your head when all about you
   Are losing theirs and blaming it on you,
If you can trust yourself when all men doubt you,
   But make allowance for their doubting too;
If you can wait and not be tired by waiting,
   Or being lied about, don't deal in lies,
Or being hated, don't give way to hating,
   And yet don't look too good, nor talk too wise:

If you can dream – and not make dreams your master;
   If you can think – and not make thoughts your aim;
If you can meet with Triumph and Disaster
   And treat those two impostors just the same;
If you can bear to hear the truth you've spoken
   Twisted by knaves to make a trap for fools,
Or watch the things you gave your life to, broken,
   And stoop and build 'em up with worn-out tools:

If you can make one heap of all your winnings
   And risk it on one turn of pitch-and-toss,
And lose, and start again at your beginnings
   And never breathe a word about your loss;
If you can force your heart and nerve and sinew
   To serve your turn long after they are gone,
And so hold on when there is nothing in you
   Except the Will which says to them: 'Hold on!'

If you can talk with crowds and keep your virtue,
   Or walk with Kings – nor lose the common touch,
If neither foes nor loving friends can hurt you,
   If all men count with you, but none too much;
If you can fill the unforgiving minute
   With sixty seconds' worth of distance run,
Yours is the Earth and everything that's in it,
   And – which is more – you'll be a Man, my son!

RUDYARD KIPLING

The Latest Decalogue

Thou shalt have one God only; who
Would be at the expense of two?
No graven images may be
Worshipped, except the currency:
Swear not at all; for for thy curse
Thine enemy is none the worse:
At church on Sunday to attend
Will serve to keep the world thy friend:
Honour thy parents; that is, all
From whom advancement may befall:
Thou shalt not kill; but needst not strive
Officiously to keep alive:
Do not adultery commit;
Advantage rarely comes of it:
Thou shalt not steal; an empty feat,
When it's so lucrative to cheat:
Bear not false witness; let the lie
Have time on its own wings to fly:
Thou shalt not covet; but tradition
Approves all forms of competition.

The sum of all is, thou shalt love,
If any body, God above:
At any rate shall never labour
More than thyself to love thy neighbour.

ARTHUR HUGH CLOUGH

Home

I Remember, I Remember

I remember, I remember,
The house where I was born,
The little window where the sun
Came peeping in at morn;
He never came a wink too soon,
Nor brought too long a day,
But now I often wish the night
Had borne my breath away!

I remember, I remember,
The roses, red and white,
The vi'lets, and the lily-cups,
Those flowers made of light!
The lilacs where the robin built,
And where my brother set
The laburnum on his birthday, –
The tree is living yet!

I remember, I remember,
Where I was used to swing,
And thought the air must rush as fresh
To swallows on the wing;
My spirit flew in feathers then,
That is so heavy now,
And summer pools could hardly cool
The fever on my brow!

I remember, I remember,
The fir trees dark and high;
I used to think their slender tops
Were close against the sky:
It was a childish ignorance,
But now 'tis little joy
To know I'm farther off from heav'n
Than when I was a boy.

THOMAS HOOD

'I vow to thee, my country'

I vow to thee, my country, all earthly things above,
Entire and whole and perfect, the service of my love:
The love that asks no question, the love that stands the test,
That lays upon the altar the dearest and the best;
The love that never falters, the love that pays the price,
The love that makes undaunted the final sacrifice.

And there's another country, I've heard of long ago,
Most dear to them that love her, most great to them that know;
We may not count her armies, we may not see her King;
Her fortress is a faithful heart, her pride is suffering;
And soul by soul and silently her shining bounds increase,
And her ways are ways of gentleness and all her paths are peace.

SIR CECIL SPRING-RICE

The Mayors

"This city & this country has brought forth many mayors,
"To sit in state & give forth laws out of their old oak chairs,
"With face as brown as any nut with drinking of strong ale;
"Good English hospitality, O then it did not fail!

"With scarlet gowns & broad gold lace would make a yeoman sweat,
"With stockings roll'd above their knees & shoes as black as jet,
"With eating beef & drinking beer, O they were stout & hale!
"Good English hospitality, O then it did not fail!

"Thus sitting at the table wide, the Mayor & Aldermen
"Were fit to give law to the city; each eat as much as ten.
"The hungry poor enter'd the hall, to eat good beef & ale.
"Good English hospitality, O then it did not fail!"

  Here they gave a shout, & the company broke up.

WILLIAM BLAKE

The Homesick Jacobite

Hame, hame, hame, O hame fain wad I be –
O hame, hame, hame, to my ain countree!

When the flower is i' the bud and the leaf is on the tree,
The larks shall sing me hame in my ain countree;
Hame, hame, hame, O hame fain wad I be –
O hame, hame, hame, to my ain countree!

The green leaf o' loyaltie's beginning for to fa',
The bonnie White Rose it is withering an' a';
But I'll water 't wi' the blude of usurping tyrannie,
An' green it will graw in my ain countree.

O, there's nocht now frae ruin my country can save,
But the keys o' kind heaven, to open the grave;
That a' the noble martyrs wha died for loyaltie
May rise again an' fight for their ain countree.

The great now are gane, a' wha ventured to save,
The new grass is springing on the tap o' their grave;
But the sun through the mirk blinks blythe in my e'e,
'I'll shine on ye yet in your ain countree.'

Hame, hame, hame, O hame fain wad I be –
O hame, hame, hame, to my ain countree!

ALLAN CUNNINGHAM

Family Court

One would be in less danger
From the wiles of a stranger
If one's own kin and kith
Were more fun to be with.

OGDEN NASH

Up at a Villa — Down in the City

(As distinguished by an Italian person of quality)

Had I but plenty of money, money enough and to spare,
The house for me, no doubt, were a house in the city-square;
Ah, such a life, such a life, as one leads at the window there!

Something to see, by Bacchus, something to hear, at least!
There, the whole day long, one's life is a perfect feast;
While up at a villa one lives, I maintain it, no more than a beast.

Well now, look at our villa! stuck like the horn of a bull
Just on a mountain's edge as bare as the creature's skull,
Save a mere shag of a bush with hardly a leaf to pull!
–I scratch my own, sometimes, to see if the hair's turned wool.

But the city, oh the city – the square with the houses! Why?
They are stone-faced, white as a curd, there 's something to take
      the eye!
Houses in four straight lines, not a single front awry;
You watch who crosses and gossips, who saunters, who hurries by;
Green blinds, as a matter of course, to draw when the sun gets
      high;
And the shops with fanciful signs which are painted properly.

What of a villa? Though winter be over in March by rights,
'T is May perhaps ere the snow shall have withered well off the
      heights:
You've the brown ploughed land before, where the oxen steam
      and wheeze,
And the hills over-smoked behind by the faint grey olive-trees.

Is it better in May, I ask you? You've summer all at once;
In a day he leaps complete with a few strong April suns.
'Mid the sharp short emerald wheat, scarce risen three fingers
      well,
The wild tulip, at end of its tube, blows out its great red bell
Like a thin clear bubble of blood, for the children to pick and sell.

Is it ever hot in the square? There's a fountain to spout and splash!
In the shade it sings and springs; in the shine such foam-bows
      flash
On the horses with curling fish-tails, that prance and paddle and
      pash

Round the lady atop in the conch – fifty gazers do not abash,
Though all that she wears is some weeds round her waist in a sort
of sash.

All the year long at the villa, nothing's to see though you linger,
Except yon cypress that points like death's lean lifted forefinger.
Some think fireflies pretty, when they mix in the corn and mingle,
Or thrid the stinking hemp till the stalks of it seem a-tingle.
Late August or early September, the stunning cicala is shrill,
And the bees keep their tiresome whine round the resinous firs
on the hill.
Enough of the seasons, – I spare you the months of the fever and
chill.

Ere opening your eyes in the city, the blessed church-bells begin:
No sooner the bells leave off, than the diligence rattles in:
You get the pick of the news, and it costs you never a pin.
By and by there's the travelling doctor gives pills, lets blood,
draws teeth;
Or the Pulcinello-trumpet breaks up the market beneath.
At the post-office such a scene-picture – the new play, piping
hot!
And a notice how, only this morning, three liberal thieves were
shot.
Above it, behold the archbishop's most fatherly of rebukes,
And beneath, with his crown and his lion, some little new law of
the Duke's!
Or a sonnet with flowery marge, to the Reverend Don So-and-so
Who is Dante, Boccaccio, Petrarca, Saint Jerome, and Cicero,
"And moreover," (the sonnet goes rhyming,) "the skirts of Saint
Paul has reached,
"Having preached us those six Lent-lectures more unctuous than
ever he preached."
Noon strikes, – here sweeps the procession! our Lady borne smiling
and smart
With a pink gauze gown all spangles, and seven swords stuck in
her heart!
Bang-whang-whang goes the drum, *tootle-le-tootle* the fife;
No keeping one's haunches still: it's the greatest pleasure in life.

But bless you, it's dear – it's dear! fowls, wine, at double the rate.
They have clapped a new tax upon salt, and what oil pays passing
the gate
It's a horror to think of. And so, the villa for me, not the city!

88

Beggars can scarcely be choosers: but still – ah, the pity, the pity!
Look, two and two go the priests, then the monks with cowls and
    sandals,
And the penitents dressed in white shirts, a-holding the yellow
    candles;
One, he carries a flap up straight, and another a cross with handles,
And the Duke's guard brings up the rear, for the better prevention
    of scandals:
Bang-whang-whang goes the drum, *tootle-te-tootle* the fife.
Oh, a day in the city-square, there is no such pleasure in life!

ROBERT BROWNING

At Lord's

It is little I repair to the matches of the Southron folk,
    Though my own red roses there may blow;
  It is little I repair to the matches of the Southron folk,
    Though the red roses crest the caps, I know.
For the field is full of shades as I near the shadowy coast,
And a ghostly batsman plays to the bowling of a ghost,
And I look through my tears on a soundless-clapping host
    As the run-stealers flicker to and fro,
        To and fro: –
  O my Hornby and my Barlow long ago!

FRANCIS THOMPSON

To S.R. Crockett

(On receiving a Dedication)

Blows the wind today, and the sun and the rain are flying,
  Blows the wind on the moors today and now,
Where about the graves of the martyrs the whaups are crying,
  My heart remembers how!

Grey recumbent tombs of the dead in desert places,
   Standing stones on the vacant wine-red moor,
Hills of sheep, and the howes of the silent vanished races,
   And winds, austere and pure:

Be it granted me to behold you again in dying,
   Hills of home! and to hear again the call;
Hear about the graves of the martyrs the peewees crying
   And hear no more at all.

ROBERT LOUIS STEVENSON

Home-Thoughts, from Abroad

Oh, to be in England
Now that April 's there,
And whoever wakes in England
Sees, some morning, unaware,
That the lowest boughs and the brushwood sheaf
Round the elm-tree bole are in tiny leaf,
While the chaffinch sings on the orchard bough
In England – now!

And after April, when May follows,
And the whitethroat builds, and all the swallows!
Hark, where my blossomed pear-tree in the hedge
Leans to the field and scatters on the clover
Blossoms and dewdrops – at the bent spray's edge –
That's the wise thrush; he sings each song twice over,
Lest you should think he never could recapture
The first fine careless rapture!
And though the fields look rough with hoary dew,
All will be gay when noontide wakes anew
The buttercups, the little children's dower
– Far brighter than this gaudy melon-flower!

ROBERT BROWNING

An Old Woman of the Roads

Oh, to have a little house!
To own the hearth and stool and all!
The heaped-up sods upon the fire,
The pile of turf against the wall!

To have a clock with weights and chains
And pendulum swinging up and down,
A dresser filled with shining delph,
Speckled and white and blue and brown!

I could be busy all the day
Clearing and sweeping hearth and floor,
And fixing on their shelf again
My white and blue and speckled store!

I could be quiet there at night
Beside the fire and by myself,
Sure of a bed and loth to leave
The ticking clock and the shining delph!

Och! but I'm weary of mist and dark,
And roads where there's never a house nor bush,
And tired I am of bog and road,
And the crying wind and the lonesome hush!

And I am praying to God on high,
And I am praying him night and day,
For a little house, a house of my own –
Out of the wind's and the rain's way.

PADRAIC COLUM

The Soldier

If I should die, think only this of me:
    That there's some corner of a foreign field
That is for ever England. There shall be
    In that rich earth a richer dust concealed;

A dust whom England bore, shaped, made aware,
   Gave, once, her flowers to love, her ways to roam,
A body of England's, breathing English air,
   Washed by the rivers, blest by suns of home.

And think, this heart, all evil shed away,
   A pulse in the eternal mind, no less
      Gives somewhere back the thoughts by England given;
Her sights and sounds; dreams happy as her day;
   And laughter, learnt of friends; and gentleness,
      In hearts at peace, under an English heaven.

RUPERT BROOKE

Empire Day

The earth is a place on which England is found,
And you find it however you twirl the globe round;
For the spots are all red and the rest is all grey,
And that is the meaning of Empire Day.

Gibraltar's a rock that you see very plain,
And attached to its base is the district of Spain.
And the island of Malta is marked further on,
Where some natives were known as the Knights of St. John.

Then Cyprus, and east to the Suez Canal,
That was conquered by Dizzy and Rothschild his pal
With the Sword of the Lord in the old English way;
And that is the meaning of Empire Day.

Our principal imports come far as Cape Horn;
For necessities, cocoa; for luxuries, corn;
Thus Brahmins are born for the rice-field, and thus,
The Gods made the Greeks to grow currants for us;
Of earth's other tributes are plenty to choose,
Tobacco and petrol and Jazzing and Jews:
The Jazzing will pass but the Jews they will stay;
And that is the meaning of Empire Day.

Our principal exports, all labelled and packed,
At the ends of the earth are delivered intact:
Our soap or our salmon can travel in tins
Between the two poles and as like as two pins;
So that Lancashire merchants whenever they like
Can water the beer of a man in Klondike
Or poison the meat of a man in Bombay;
And that is the meaning of Empire Day.

The day of St. George is a musty affair
Which Russians and Greeks are permitted to share;
The day of Trafalgar is Spanish in name
And the Spaniards refuse to pronounce it the same;
But the day of the Empire from Canada came
With Morden and Borden and Beaverbrook's fame
And saintly seraphical souls such as they:
And that is the meaning of Empire Day.

G.K. CHESTERTON

The Land

When Julius Fabricius, Sub-Prefect of the Weald,
In the days of Diocletian owned our Lower River-field,
He called to him Hobdenius – a Briton of the Clay,
Saying: 'What about that River-piece for layin' in to hay?'

And the aged Hobden answered: 'I remember as a lad
My father told your father that she wanted dreenin' bad.
An' the more that you neeglect her the less you'll get her clean.
Have it jest *as* you've a mind to, but, if I was you, I'd dreen.'

So they drained it long and crossways in the lavish Roman style.
Still we find among the river-drift their flakes of ancient tile,
And in drouthy middle August, when the bones of meadows show,
We can trace the lines they followed sixteen hundred years ago.

Then Julius Fabricius died as even Prefects do,
And after certain centuries, Imperial Rome died too.
Then did robbers enter Britain from across the Northern main
And our Lower River-field was won by Ogier the Dane.

Well could Ogier work his war-boat – well could Ogier wield his
  brand –
Much he knew of foaming waters – not so much of farming land.
So he called to him a Hobden of the old unaltered blood,
Saying: 'What about that River-bit, she doesn't look no good?'

And that aged Hobden answered: ''Tain't for *me* to interfere,
But I've known that bit o' meadow now for five and fifty year.
Have it *jest* as you've a mind to, but I've proved it time on time,
If you want to change her nature you have *got* to give her lime!'

Ogier sent his wains to Lewes, twenty hours' solemn walk,
And drew back great abundance of the cool, grey, healing chalk.
And old Hobden spread it broadcast, never heeding what was in't;
Which is why in cleaning ditches, now and then we find a flint.

Ogier died. His sons grew English. Anglo-Saxon was their name,
Till out of blossomed Normandy another pirate came;
For Duke William conquered England and divided with his men,
And our Lower River-field he gave to William of Warenne.

But the Brook (you know her habit) rose one rainy Autumn night
And tore down sodden flitches of the bank to left and right.
So, said William to his Bailiff as they rode their dripping rounds:
'Hob, what about that River-bit – the Brook's got up no bounds?'

And that aged Hobden answered: ''Tain't my business to advise,
But ye might ha' known 'twould happen from the way the valley
  lies.
When ye can't hold back the water you must try and save the sile.
Hev it jest as you've a *mind* to, but, if I was you, I'd spile!'

They spiled along the water-course with trunks of willow-trees
And planks of elms behind 'em and immortal oaken knees.
And when the spates of Autumn whirl the gravel-beds away
You can see their faithful fragments iron-hard in iron clay.

.   .   .   .   .   .

Georgii Quinti Anno Sexto, I, who own the River-field,
Am fortified with title-deeds, attested, signed and sealed,
Guaranteeing me, my assigns, my executors and heirs
All sorts of powers and profits which – are neither mine nor theirs.

I have rights of chase and warren, as my dignity requires.
I can fish – but Hobden tickles. I can shoot – but Hobden wires.
I repair, but he reopens, certain gaps which, men allege,
Have been used by every Hobden since a Hobden swapped a
    hedge.

Shall I dog his morning progress o'er the track-betraying dew?
Demand his dinner-basket into which my pheasant flew?
Confiscate his evening faggot into which the conies ran,
And summons him to judgment? I would sooner summons Pan.

His dead are in the churchyard – thirty generations laid.
Their names went down in Domesday Book when Domesday
    Book was made.
And the passion and the piety and prowess of his line
Have seeded, rooted, fruited in some land the Law calls mine.

Not for any beast that burrows, nor for any bird that flies,
Would I lose his large sound counsel, miss his keen amending
    eyes.
He is bailiff, woodman, wheelwright, field-surveyor, engineer,
And if flagrantly a poacher – 'tain't for me to interfere.

'Hob, what about that River-bit?' I turn to him again
With Fabricius and Ogier and William of Warenne.
'Hev it jest as you've a mind to, *but*' – and so he takes command.
For whoever pays the taxes old Mus' Hobden owns the land.

RUDYARD KIPLING

Distances

Tarantella

Do you remember an Inn,
Miranda?
Do you remember an Inn?
And the tedding and the spreading
Of the straw for a bedding,
And the fleas that tease in the High Pyrenees,
And the wine that tasted of the tar?
And the cheers and the jeers of the young muleteers
(Under the vine of the dark verandah)?
Do you remember an Inn, Miranda,
Do you remember an Inn?
And the cheers and the jeers of the young muleteers
Who hadn't got a penny,
And who weren't paying any,
And the hammer at the doors and the Din?
And the Hip! Hop! Hap!
Of the clap
Of the hands to the twirl and the swirl
Of the girl gone chancing,
Glancing,
Dancing,
Backing and advancing,
Snapping of a clapper to the spin
Out and in –
And the Ting, Tong, Tang of the Guitar!
Do you remember an Inn,
Miranda?
Do you remember an Inn?

Never more;
Miranda,
Never more.
Only the high peaks hoar:
And Aragon a torrent at the door.
No sound
In the walls of the Halls where falls

96

The tread
Of the feet of the dead to the ground
No sound:
But the boom
Of the far Waterfall like Doom.

HILAIRE BELLOC

Bermudas

Where the remote Bermudas ride
In th' oceans' bosom unespyed,
From a small boat that rowed along,
The listning winds received this song.
    What should we do but sing His praise
That led us through the watry maze,
Unto an Isle so long unknown,
And yet far kinder than our own?
Where He the huge sea-monsters wracks,
That lift the deep upon their backs.
He lands us on a grassy stage;
Safe from the storms, and prelates' rage.
He gave us this eternal spring,
Which here enamels every thing;
And sends the fowls to us in care,
On daily visits through the air.
He hangs in shades the orange bright,
Like golden lamps in a green night.
And does in the pomgranates close,
Jewels more rich than Ormus shows.
He makes the figs our mouths to meet;
And throws the melons at our feet.
But apples plants of such a price,
No tree could ever bear them twice.
With cedars chosen by His hand,
From Lebanon, He stores the land.
And makes the hollow seas, that roar,
Proclaim the ambergris on shore.
He cast (of which we rather boast)
The Gospels' pearl upon our coast.
And in these rocks for us did frame

A temple, where to sound His name.
Oh let our voice His praise exalt,
Till it arrive at Heaven's vault:
Which thence (perhaps) rebounding, may
Echo beyond the Mexique Bay.
Thus sung they, in the English boat,
An holy and a cheerful note,
And all the way, to guide their chime,
With falling oars they kept the time.

ANDREW MARVELL

Gypsies in the Wood

My mother said that I never should
Play with the gypsies in the wood,
The wood was dark; the grass was green;
In came Sally with a tambourine,
I went to the sea – no ship to get across;
I paid ten shillings for a blind white horse;
I up on his back and was off in a crack,
Sally, tell my Mother I shall never come back.

ANON

Arabia

Far as the shades of Arabia,
   Where the Princes ride at noon,
'Mid the verdurous vales and thickets,
   Under the ghost of the moon;
And so dark is that vaulted purple
   Flowers in the forest rise
And toss into blossom 'gainst the phantom stars
   Pale in the noonday skies.

Sweet is the music of Arabia
　　In my heart, when out of dreams
I still in the thin clear mirk of dawn
　　Descry her gliding streams;
Hear her strange lutes on the green banks
　　Ring loud with the grief and delight
Of the dim-silked, dark-haired Musicians
　　In the brooding silence of night.

They haunt me – her lutes and her forests;
　　No beauty on earth I see
But shadowed with that dream recalls
　　Her loveliness to me:
Still eyes look coldly upon me,
　　Cold voices whisper and say –
'He is crazed with the spell of far Arabia,
　　They have stolen his wits away.'

WALTER DE LA MARE

Italia, io ti saluto

To come back from the sweet South, to the North
　　Where I was born, bred, look to die;
Come back to do my day's work in its day,
　　Play out my play –
　　Amen, amen, say I.

To see no more the country half my own,
　　Nor hear the half familiar speech,
Amen, I say; I turn to that bleak North
　　Whence I came forth –
　　The South lies out of reach.

But when our swallows fly back to the South,
　　To the sweet South, to the sweet South,
The tears may come again into my eyes
　　On the old wise,
　　And the sweet name to my mouth.

CHRISTINA ROSSETTI

99

Sea-Fever

I must go down to the seas again, to the lonely sea and the sky,
And all I ask is a tall ship and a star to steer her by,
And the wheel's kick and the wind's song and the white sail's
    shaking,
And a grey mist on the sea's face and a grey dawn breaking.

I must go down to the seas again, for the call of the running tide
Is a wild call and a clear call that may not be denied;
And all I ask is a windy day with the white clouds flying,
And the flung spray and the blown spume and the sea-gulls
    crying.

I must go down to the seas again to the vagrant gypsy life,
To the gull's way and the whale's way where the wind's like a
    whetted knife;
And all I ask is a merry yarn from a laughing fellow-rover,
And quiet sleep and a sweet dream when the long trick's over.

JOHN MASEFIELD

On First Looking into Chapman's Homer

Much have I travelled in the realms of gold,
    And many goodly states and kingdoms seen;
    Round many western islands have I been
Which bards in fealty to Apollo hold.
Oft of one wide expanse had I been told
    That deep-browed Homer ruled as his demesne;
    Yet did I never breathe its pure serene
Till I heard Chapman speak out loud and bold.
Then felt I like some watcher of the skies
    When a new planet swims into his ken;
Or like stout Cortez when with eagle eyes
    He stared at the Pacific, and all his men
Looked at each other with a wild surmise –
    Silent, upon a peak in Darien.

JOHN KEATS

Mandalay

By the old Moulmein Pagoda, lookin' lazy at the sea,
There's a Burma girl a-settin', and I know she thinks o' me;
For the wind is in the palm-trees, and the temple-bells they say:
'Come you back, you British soldier; come you back to Mandalay!'
>Come you back to Mandalay,
>Where the old Flotilla lay:
>Can't you 'ear their paddles chunkin' from Rangoon to
>Mandalay?
>On the road to Mandalay,
>Where the flyin'-fishes play,
>An' the dawn comes up like thunder outer China 'crost
>the Bay!

'Er petticoat was yaller an' 'er little cap was green,
An' 'er name was Supi-yaw-lat – jes' the same as Theebaw's Queen,
An' I seed her first a-smokin' of a whackin' white cheroot,
An' a-wastin' Christian kisses on an 'eathen idol's foot:
>Bloomin' idol made o' mud –
>Wot they called the Great Gawd Budd –
>Plucky lot she cared for idols when I kissed 'er where
>she stud!
>On the road to Mandalay...

When the mist was on the rice-fields an' the sun was droppin' slow,
She'd git 'er little banjo an' she'd sing *'Kulla-lo-lo!'*
With 'er arm upon my shoulder an' 'er cheek agin my cheek
We useter watch the steamers an' the *hathis* pilin' teak.
>Elephints a-pilin' teak
>In the sludgy, squdgy creek,
>Where the silence 'ung that 'eavy you was 'arf afraid to
>speak!
>On the road to Mandalay...

But that's all shove be'ind me – long ago an' fur away,
An' there ain't no 'buses runnin' from the Bank to Mandalay;
An' I'm learnin' 'ere in London what the ten-year soldier tells:
'If you've 'eard the East a-callin', you won't never 'eed naught else.'
>No! you won't 'eed nothin' else
>But them spicy garlic smells,
>An' the sunshine an' the palm-trees an' the tinkly temple-
>bells;
>On the road to Mandalay...

I am sick o' wastin' leather on these gritty pavin'-stones,
An' the blasted English drizzle wakes the fever in my bones;
Tho' I walks with fifty 'ousemaids outer Chelsea to the Strand,
An' they talks a lot o' lovin', but wot do they understand?
     Beefy face an' grubby 'and –
     Law! wot do they understand?
     I've a neater, sweeter maiden in a cleaner, greener land!
     On the road to Mandalay...

Ship me somewheres east of Suez, where the best is like the
    worst,
Where there aren't no Ten Commandments an' a man can raise a
    thirst;
For the temple-bells are callin', an' it's there that I would be –
By the old Moulmein Pagoda, looking lazy at the sea;
     On the road to Mandalay,
     Where the old Flotilla lay,
     With our sick beneath the awnings when we went to
       Mandalay!
     O the road to Mandalay,
     Where the flyin'-fishes play,
     An' the dawn comes up like thunder outer China 'crost
       the Bay!

RUDYARD KIPLING

The Lake Isle of Innisfree

I will arise and go now, and go to Innisfree,
And a small cabin build there, of clay and wattles made:
Nine bean-rows will I have there, a hive for the honey-bee,
And live alone in the bee-loud glade.

And I shall have some peace there, for peace comes dropping
    slow,
Dropping from the veils of the morning to where the cricket
    sings;
There midnight's all a glimmer, and noon a purple glow,
And evening full of the linnet's wings.

I will arise and go now, for always night and day
I hear lake water lapping with low sounds by the shore;
While I stand on the roadway, or on the pavements grey,
I hear it in the deep heart's core.

W.B. YEATS

The Golden Journey to Samarkand

Prologue

We who with songs beguile your pilgrimage
　　And swear that Beauty lives though lilies die,
We Poets of the proud old lineage
　　Who sing to find your hearts, we know not why, –

What shall we tell you? Tales, marvellous tales
　　Of ships and stars and isles where good men rest,
Where nevermore the rose of sunset pales,
　　And winds and shadows fall toward the West:

And there the world's first huge white-bearded kings
　　In dim glades sleeping, murmur in their sleep,
And closer round their breasts the ivy clings,
　　Cutting its pathway slow and red and deep.

II

And how beguile you? Death has no repose
　　Warmer and deeper than that Orient sand
Which hides the beauty and bright faith of those
　　Who made the Golden Journey to Samarkand.

And now they wait and whiten peaceably,
　　Those conquerors, those poets, those so fair:
They know time comes, not only you and I,
　　But the whole world shall whiten, here or there;

When those long caravans that cross the plain
　　With dauntless feet and sound of silver bells
Put forth no more for glory or for gain,
　　Take no more solace from the palm-girt wells.

When the great markets by the sea shut fast
  All that calm Sunday that goes on and on:
When even lovers find their peace at last,
  And Earth is but a star, that once had shone.

JAMES ELROY FLECKER

The Rolling English Road

Before the Roman came to Rye or out to Severn strode,
The rolling English drunkard made the rolling English road.
A reeling road, a rolling road, that rambles round the shire,
And after him the parson ran, the sexton and the squire;
A merry road, a mazy road, and such as we did tread
The night we went to Birmingham by way of Beachy Head.

I knew no harm of Bonaparte and plenty of the Squire,
And for to fight the Frenchman I did not much desire;
But I did bash their baggonets because they came arrayed
To straighten out the crooked road an English drunkard made,
Where you and I went down the lane with ale-mugs in our hands,
The night we went to Glastonbury by way of Goodwin Sands.

His sins they were forgiven him; or why do flowers run
Behind him; and the hedges all strengthening in the sun?
The wild thing went from left to right and knew not which was
    which,
But the wild rose was above him when they found him in the ditch.
God pardon us, nor harden us; we did not see so clear
The night we went to Bannockburn by way of Brighton Pier.

My friends, we will not go again or ape an ancient rage,
Or stretch the folly of our youth to be the shame of age,
But walk with clearer eyes and ears this path that wandereth,
And see undrugged in evening light the decent inn of death;
For there is good news yet to hear and fine things to be seen,
Before we go to Paradise by way of Kensal Green.

G.K. CHESTERTON

Romance

When I was but thirteen or so
  I went into a golden land;
Chimborazo, Cotopaxi
  Took me by the hand.

My father died, my brother too,
  They passed like fleeting dreams,
I stood where Popocatapetl
  In the sunlight gleams.

I dimly heard the master's voice
  And boys far-off at play;
Chimborazo, Cotopaxi
  Had stolen me away.

I walked in a great golden dream
  To and fro from school –
Shining Popocatapetl
  The dusty streets did rule.

I walked home with a gold dark boy
  And never a word I'd say;
Chimborazo, Cotopaxi
  Had taken my speech away:

I gazed entranced upon his face
  Fairer than any flower –
O shining Popocatapetl,
  It was thy magic hour:

The houses, people, traffic seemed
  Thin fading dreams by day;
Chimborazo, Cotopaxi,
  They had stolen my soul away!

W.J. TURNER

Where do the gipsies come from?

Where do the gipsies come from?
The gipsies come from Egypt.
The fiery sun begot them,
  Their dam was the desert dry.
She lay there stripped and basking,
And gave them suck for the asking,
And an Emperor's bone to play with,
  Whenever she heard them cry.

What did the gipsies do there?
They built a tomb for Pharaoh,
They built a tomb for Pharaoh,
  So tall it touched the sky.
They buried him deep inside it,
Then let what would betide it,
They saddled their lean-ribbed ponies
  And left him there to die.

What do the gipsies do now?
They follow the Sun, their father,
They follow the Sun, their father,
  They know not whither nor why.
Whatever they find they take it,
And if it's a law they break it.
So never you talk to a gipsy,
  Or look in a gipsy's eye.

H.H. BASHFORD

'How many miles to Babylon?'

How many miles to Babylon?
Three score miles and ten.
Can I get there by candle-light?
Yes, and back again!

ANON

Open Air

Pippa's Song

The year's at the spring,
And day's at the morn;
Morning's at seven;
The hill-side's dew-pearled;
The lark's on the wing;
The snail's on the thorn:
God's in his heaven –
All's right with the world!

ROBERT BROWNING

The Question

I dreamed that, as I wandered by the way,
　　Bare Winter suddenly was changed to Spring,
And gentle odours led my steps astray,
　　Mixed with a sound of waters murmuring
Along a shelving bank of turf, which lay
　　Under a copse, and hardly dared to fling
Its green arms round the bosom of the stream,
But kissed it and then fled, as thou mightest in dream.

There grew pied wind-flowers and violets,
　　Daisies, those pearled Arcturi of the earth,
The constellated flower that never sets;
　　Faint oxslips; tender bluebells, at whose birth
The sod scarce heaved; and that tall flower that wets –
　　Like a child, half in tenderness and mirth –
Its mother's face with Heaven's collected tears,
When the low wind, its playmate's voice, it hears.

And in the warm hedge grew lush eglantine,
  Green cowbind and the moonlight-coloured may,
And cherry-blossoms, and white cups, whose wine
  Was the bright dew, yet drained not by the day;
And wild roses, and ivy serpentine,
  With its dark buds and leaves, wandering astray;
And flowers azure, black, and streaked with gold,
Fairer than any wakened eyes behold.

And nearer to the river's trembling edge
  There grew broad flag-flowers, purple pranked with white,
And starry river buds among the sedge,
  And floating water-lilies, broad and bright,
Which lit the oak that overhung the hedge
  With moonlight beams of their own watery light;
And bulrushes, and reeds of such deep green
As soothed the dazzled eye with sober sheen.

Methought that of these visionary flowers
  I made a nosegay, bound in such a way
That the same hues, which in their natural bowers
  Were mingled or opposed, the like array
Kept these imprisoned children of the Hours
  Within my hand, – and then, elate and gay,
I hastened to the spot whence I had come,
That I might there present it! – Oh! to whom?

PERCY BYSSHE SHELLEY

Leisure

What is this life if, full of care,
We have no time to stand and stare.

No time to stand beneath the boughs
And stare as long as sheep or cows.

No time to see, when woods we pass,
Where squirrels hide their nuts in grass.

No time to see, in broad daylight,
Streams full of stars like skies at night.

No time to turn at Beauty's glance,
And watch her feet, how they can dance.

No time to wait till her mouth can
Enrich that smile her eyes began.

A poor life this if, full of care,
We have no time to stand and stare.

W.H. DAVIES

Mending Wall

Something there is that doesn't love a wall,
That sends the frozen-ground-swell under it
And spills the upper boulders in the sun,
And makes gaps even two can pass abreast.
The work of hunters is another thing:
I have come after them and made repair
Where they have left not one stone on a stone,
But they would have the rabbit out of hiding,
To please the yelping dogs. The gaps I mean,
No one has seen them made or heard them made,
But at spring mending-time we find them there.
I let my neighbor know beyond the hill;
And on a day we meet to walk the line
And set the wall between us once again.
We keep the wall between us as we go.
To each the boulders that have fallen to each.
And some are loaves and some so nearly balls
We have to use a spell to make them balance:
'Stay where you are until our backs are turned!'
We wear our fingers rough with handling them.
Oh, just another kind of outdoor game,
One on a side. It comes to little more:
There where it is we do not need the wall:
He is all pine and I am apple orchard.
My apple trees will never get across

And eat the cones under his pines, I tell him.
He only says, 'Good fences make good neighbors.'
Spring is the mischief in me, and I wonder
If I could put a notion in his head:
'Why do they make good neighbors? Isn't it
Where there are cows? But here there are no cows.
Before I built a wall I'd ask to know
What I was walling in or walling out,
And to whom I was like to give offense,
Something there is that doesn't love a wall,
That wants it down.' I could say 'Elves' to him,
But it's not elves exactly, and I'd rather
He said it for himself. I see him there,
Bringing a stone grasped firmly by the top
In each hand, like an old-stone savage armed.
He moves in darkness as it seems to me,
Not of woods only and the shade of trees.
He will not go behind his father's saying.
And he likes having thought of it so well
He says again, 'Good fences make good neighbors.'

ROBERT FROST

Composed upon Westminster Bridge, September 3, 1802

Earth has not anything to show more fair:
Dull would he be of soul who could pass by
A sight so touching in its majesty:
This City now doth, like a garment, wear
The beauty of the morning; silent, bare,
Ships, towers, domes, theatres, and temples lie
Open unto the fields, and to the sky;
All bright and glittering in the smokeless air.
Never did sun more beautifully steep
In his first splendour, valley, rock, or hill;
Ne'er saw I, never felt, a calm so deep!
The river glideth at his own sweet will:
Dear God! the very houses seem asleep;
And all that mighty heart is lying still!

WILLIAM WORDSWORTH

Stopping by Woods on a Snowy Evening

Whose woods these are I think I know.
His house is in the village, though;
He will not see me stopping here
To watch his woods fill up with snow.

My little horse must think it queer
To stop without a farmhouse near
Between the woods and frozen lake
The darkest evening of the year.

He gives his harness bells a shake
To ask if there is some mistake.
The only other sound's the sweep
Of easy wind and downy flake.

The woods are lovely, dark, and deep,
But I have promises to keep,
And miles to go before I sleep,
And miles to go before I sleep.

ROBERT FROST

To Autumn

Season of mists and mellow fruitfulness,
  Close bosom friend of the maturing sun,
Conspiring with him how to load and bless
  With fruit the vines that round the thatch-eves run:
To bend with apples the mossed cottage-trees,
  And fill all fruit with ripeness to the core;
    To swell the gourd, and plump the hazel shells
  With a sweet kernel; to set budding more,
And still more, later flowers for the bees,
Until they think warm days will never cease,
    For summer has o'er-brimmed their clammy cells.

Who hath not seen thee oft amid thy store?
　　Sometimes whoever seeks abroad may find
Thee sitting careless on a granary floor,
　　Thy hair soft-lifted by the winnowing wind;
Or on a half-reaped furrow sound asleep,
　　Drowsed with the fume of poppies, while thy hook
　　　Spares the next swath and all its twinèd flowers;
And sometimes like a gleaner thou dost keep
　　Steady thy laden head across a brook;
　　Or by a cyder-press, with patient look,
　　　Thou watchest the last oozings hours by hours.

Where are the songs of spring? Aye, where are they?
　　Think not of them, thou hast thy music too –
While barrèd clouds bloom the soft-dying day,
　　And touch the stubble-plains with rosy hue.
Then in a wailful choir the small gnats mourn
　　Among the river sallows, borne aloft
　　　Or sinking as the light wind lives or dies;
And full-grown lambs loud bleat from hilly bourn;
　　Hedge-crickets sing; and now with treble soft
　　The red-breast whistles from a garden-croft;
　　　And gathering swallows twitter in the skies.

JOHN KEATS

The Reverie of Poor Susan

At the corner of Wood Street, when daylight appears,
Hangs a Thrush that sings loud, it has sung for three years:
Poor Susan has passed by the spot, and has heard
In the silence of morning the song of the Bird.

'Tis a note of enchantment; what ails her? She sees
A mountain ascending, a vision of trees;
Bright volumes of vapour through Lothbury glide,
And a river flows on through the vale of Cheapside.

Green pastures she views in the midst of the dale,
Down which she so often has tripped with her pail;

And a single small cottage, a nest like a dove's,
The one only dwelling on earth that she loves.

She looks, and her heart is in heaven: but they fade,
The mist and the river, the hill and the shade:
The stream will not flow, and the hill will not rise,
And the colours have all passed away from her eyes!

WILLIAM WORDSWORTH

'Here we come a-piping'

Here we come a-piping,
In Springtime and in May;
Green fruit a-ripening,
And Winter fled away.

The Queen she sits upon the strand,
Fair as lily, white as wand;
Seven billows on the sea,
Horses riding fast and free,
And bells beyond the sand.

ANON

A Boy's Song

Where the pools are bright and deep
Where the grey trout lies asleep
Up the river and o'er the lea
That's the way for Billy and me

Where the blackbird sings the latest
Where the hawthorn blooms the sweetest
Where the nestlings plentiest be
That's the way for Billy and me

Where the mowers mow the cleanest
Where the hay lies thick and greenest
There to trace the homeward bee
That's the way for Billy and me

Where the poplar grows the smallest
Where the old pine waves the tallest
Pies and rooks know who are we
That's the way for Billy and me

Where the hazel bank is steepest
Where the shadow falls the deepest
There the clustering nuts fall free
That's the way for Billy and me

Why the boys should drive away
Little sweet maidens from the play
Or love to tear and fight so well
That's the thing I never could tell

But this I know I love to play
Through the meadow among the hay
Up the water and o'er the lea
That's the way for Billy and me

JAMES HOGG

A Widow Bird

A widow bird sate mourning for her love
    Upon a wintry bough;
The frozen wind crept on above,
    The freezing stream below.

There was no leaf upon the forest bare,
    No flower upon the ground,
And little motion in the air
    Except the mill-wheel's sound.

PERCY BYSSHE SHELLEY

Poor Beasts

The Bells of Heaven

'Twould ring the bells of Heaven
The wildest peal for years,
If Parson lost his senses
And people came to theirs,
And he and they together
Knelt down with angry prayers
For tamed and shabby tigers
And dancing dogs and bears,
And wretched, blind pit ponies,
And little hunted hares.

RALPH HODGSON

'I had a dove and the sweet dove died'

I had a dove and the sweet dove died,
  And I have thought it died of grieving.
Oh, what could it grieve for? Its feet were tied
  With a silken thread of my own hand's weaving.
Sweet little red feet! Why should you die –
Why would you leave me, sweet dove! Why?
You lived alone on the forest-tree,
Why, pretty thing, could you not live with me?
I kissed you oft and gave you white peas;
Why not live sweetly, as in the green trees?

JOHN KEATS

Eddi's Service

Eddi, priest of St Wilfrid
  In the chapel at Manhood End,
Ordered a midnight service
  For such as cared to attend.

But the Saxons were keeping Christmas,
  And the night was stormy as well.
Nobody came to service
  Though Eddi rang the bell.

'Wicked weather for walking,'
  Said Eddi of Manhood End.
'But I must go on with the service
  For such as care to attend.'

The altar candles were lighted, –
  An old marsh donkey came,
Bold as a guest invited,
  And stared at the guttering flame.

The storm beat on at the windows,
  The water splashed on the floor,
And a wet yoke-weary bullock
  Pushed in through the open door.

'How do I know what is greatest,
  How do I know what is least?
That is My Father's business.'
  Said Eddi, Wilfrid's priest.

'But, three are gathered together –
  Listen to me and attend.
I bring good news, my brethren!'
  Said Eddi, of Manhood End.

And he told the Ox of a manger
  And a stall in Bethlehem,
And he spoke to the Ass of a Rider
  That rode to Jerusalem.

They steamed and dripped in the chancel,
    They listened and never stirred,
While, just as though they were Bishops,
    Eddi preached them The Word.

Till the gale blew off on the marshes
    And the windows showed the day,
And the Ox and the Ass together
    Wheeled and clattered away.

And when the Saxons mocked him,
    Said Eddi of Manhood End,
'I dare not shut His chapel
    On such as care to attend.'

                    RUDYARD KIPLING

The Snare

I hear a sudden cry of pain!
There is a rabbit in a snare:
Now I hear the cry again,
But I cannot tell from where.

But I cannot tell from where
He is calling out for aid!
Crying on the frightened air,
Making everything afraid!

Making everything afraid!
Wrinkling up his little face!
As he cries again for aid;
– And I cannot find the place!

And I cannot find the place
Where his paw is in the snare!
Little One! Oh, Little One!
I am searching everywhere!

                    JAMES STEPHENS

An Elegy on the Death of a Mad Dog

Good people all, of every sort,
   Give ear unto my song;
And if you find it wond'rous short,
   It cannot hold you long.

In Isling town there was a man,
   Of whom the world might say,
That still a godly race he ran,
   Whene'er he went to pray.

A kind and gentle heart he had,
   To comfort friends and foes;
The naked every day he clad,
   When he put on his cloaths.

And in that town a dog was found,
   As many dogs there be,
Both mungrel, puppy, whelp, and hound,
   And curs of low degree.

This dog and man at first were friends;
   But when a pique began,
The dog, to gain some private ends,
   Went mad and bit the man.

Around from all the neighbouring streets,
   The wondering neighbours ran,
And swore the dog had lost his wits,
   To bite so good a man.

The wound it seem'd both sore and sad,
   To every christian eye;
And while they swore the dog was mad,
   They swore the man would die.

But soon a wonder came to light,
   That shew'd the rogues they lied,
The man recovered of the bite,
   The dog it was that dy'd.

OLIVER GOLDSMITH

Auguries of Innocence

To see a World in a Grain of Sand
And a Heaven in a Wild Flower,
Hold Infinity in the palm of your hand
And Eternity in an hour.

A Robin Red breast in a Cage
Puts all Heaven in a Rage.
A dove house fill'd with doves & Pigeons
Shudders Hell thro' all its regions.
A dog starv'd at his Master's Gate
Predicts the ruin of the State.
A Horse misus'd upon the Road
Calls to Heaven for Human blood.
Each outcry of the hunted Hare
A fibre from the Brain does tear.
A Skylark wounded in the wing,
A Cherubim does cease to sing.
The Game Cock clip'd & arm'd for fight
Does the Rising Sun affright.
Every Wolf's & Lion's howl
Raises from Hell a Human Soul.
The wild deer, wand'ring here & there,
Keeps the Human Soul from Care.
The Lamb misus'd breeds Public strife
And yet forgives the Butcher's Knife.
The Bat that flits at close of Eve
Has left the Brain that won't Believe.
The Owl that calls upon the Night
Speaks the Unbeliever's fright.
He who shall hurt the little Wren
Shall never be belov'd by Men.
He who the Ox to wrath has mov'd
Shall never be by Woman lov'd.
The wanton Boy that kills the Fly
Shall feel the Spider's enmity.
He who torments the Chafer's sprite
Weaves a Bower in endless Night.
The Catterpiller on the Leaf
Repeats to thee thy Mother's grief.
Kill not the Moth nor Butterfly,
For the Last Judgment draweth nigh.
He who shall train the Horse to War

Shall never pass the Polar Bar.
The Begger's Dog & Widow's Cat,
Feed them & thou wilt grow fat.
The Gnat that sings his Summer's song
Poison gets from Slander's tongue.
The poison of the Snake & Newt
Is the sweat of Envy's Foot.
The poison of the Honey Bee
Is the Artist's Jealousy.
The Prince's Robes & Beggar's Rags
Are Toadstools on the Miser's Bags.
A truth that's told with bad intent
Beats all the Lies you can invent.
It is right it should be so;
Man was made for Joy & Woe;
And when this we rightly know
Thro' the World we safely go.

WILLIAM BLAKE

A Runnable Stag

When the pods went pop on the broom, green broom,
  And apples began to be golden-skinned,
We harboured a stag in the Priory coomb,
  And we feathered his trail up-wind, up-wind,
  We feathered his trail up-wind –
    A stag of warrant, a stag, a stag,
    A runnable stag, a kingly crop,
    Brow, bay and tray and three on top,
    A stag, a runnable stag.

Then the huntsman's horn rang yap, yap, yap,
  And 'Forwards' we heard the harbourer shout;
But 'twas only a brocket that broke a gap
  In the beechen underwood, driven out,
  From the underwood antlered out
    By warrant and might of the stag, the stag,
    The runnable stag, whose lordly mind
    Was bent on sleep, though beamed and tined
    He stood, a runnable stag.

So we tufted the covert till afternoon
    With Tinkerman's Pup and Bell-of-the-North;
And hunters were sulky and hounds out of tune
    Before we tufted the right stag forth,
    Before we tufted him forth,
        The stag of warrant, the wily stag,
        The runnable stag with his kingly crop,
        Brow, bay and tray and three on top,
        The royal and runnable stag.

It was Bell-of-the-North and Tinkerman's Pup
    That stuck to the scent till the copse was drawn.
'Tally ho! tally ho!' and the hunt was up,
    The tufters whipped and the pack laid on,
    The resolute pack laid on,
        And the stag of warrant away at last,
        The runnable stag, the same, the same,
        His hoofs on fire, his horns like flame,
        A stag, a runnable stag.

'Let your gelding be: if you check or chide
    He stumbles at once and you're out of the hunt;
For three hundred gentlemen, able to ride,
    On hunters accustomed to bear the brunt,
    Accustomed to bear the brunt,
        Are after the runnable stag, the stag,
        The runnable stag with his kingly crop,   ·
        Brow, bay and tray and three on top,
        The right, the runnable stag.'

By perilous paths in coomb and dell,
    The heather, the rocks, and the river-bed,
The pace grew hot, for the scent lay well,
    And a runnable stag goes right ahead,
    The quarry went right ahead –
        Ahead, ahead, and fast and far;
        His antlered crest, his cloven hoof,
        Brow, bay and tray and three aloof,
        The stag, the runnable stag.

For a matter of twenty miles and more,
    By the densest hedge and the highest wall,
Through herds of bullocks he baffled the lore
    Of harbourer, huntsman, hounds and all,

Of harbourer, hounds and all –
   The stag of warrant, the wily stag,
   For twenty miles, and five and five,
   He ran, and he never was caught alive,
   This stag, this runnable stag.

When he turned at bay in the leafy gloom,
  In the emerald gloom where the brook ran deep,
He heard in the distance the rollers boom,
  And he saw in a vision a peaceful sleep,
  In a wonderful vision of sleep,
   A stag of warrant, a stag, a stag,
   A runnable stag in a jewelled bed,
   Under the sheltering ocean dead,
   A stag, a runnable stag.

So a fateful hope lit up his eye,
  And he opened his nostrils wide again,
And he tossed his branching antlers high
  As he headed the hunt down the Charlock glen,
  As he raced down the echoing glen,
   For five miles more, the stag, the stag,
   For twenty miles, and five and five,
   Not to be caught now, dead or alive,
   The stag, the runnable stag.

Three hundred gentlemen, able to ride,
  Three hundred horses as gallant and free,
Behind him escape on the evening tide,
  Far out till he sank in the Severn Sea,
  Till he sank in the depths of the sea –
   The stag, the buoyant stag, the stag
   That slept at last in a jewelled bed
   Under the sheltering ocean spread,
   The stag, the runnable stag.

JOHN DAVIDSON

from *Reynard the Fox*

The fox he was strong, he was full of running,
He could run for an hour and then be cunning,
But the cry behind him made him chill,
They were nearer now and they meant to kill.
They meant to run him until his blood
Clogged on his heart as his brush with mud,
Till his back bent up and his tongue hung flagging,
And his belly and brush were filthed from dragging.
Till he crouched stone still, dead-beat and dirty,
With nothing but teeth against the thirty.
And all the way to that blinding end
He would meet with men and have none his friend.
Men to holloa and men to run him,
With stones to stagger and yells to stun him,
Men to head him, with whips to beat him,
Teeth to mangle and mouths to eat him.
And all the way, that wild high crying,
To cold his blood with the thought of dying,
The horn and the cheer, and the drum-like thunder,
Of the horse hooves stamping the meadows under.
He upped his brush and went with a will
For the Sarsen Stones on Wan Dyke Hill.

JOHN MASEFIELD

Done For

Old Ben Bailey
He's been and done
For a small brown bunny
With his long gun.

Glazed are the eyes
That stared so clear,
And no sound stirs
In that hairy ear.

What was once beautiful
Now breathes not,
Bound for Ben Bailey's
Smoking pot.

WALTER DE LA MARE

The Runaway

Once when the snow of the year was beginning to fall,
We stopped by a mountain pasture to say, 'Whose colt?'
A little Morgan had one forefoot on the wall,
The other curled at his breast. He dipped his head
And snorted at us. And then he had to bolt.
We heard the miniature thunder where he fled,
And we saw him, or thought we saw him, dim and gray,
Like a shadow against the curtain of falling flakes.
'I think the little fellow's afraid of the snow.
He isn't winter-broken. It isn't play
With the little fellow at all. He's running away.
I doubt if even his mother could tell him, "Sakes,
It's only weather." He'd think she didn't know!
Where is his mother? He can't be out alone.'
And now he comes again with clatter of stone,
And mounts the wall again with whited eyes
And all his tail that isn't hair up straight.
He shudders his coat as if to throw off flies.
'Whoever it is that leaves him out so late,
When other creatures have gone to stall and bin,
Ought to be told to come and take him in.'

ROBERT FROST

The Irish Harper and his Dog

On the green banks of Shannon, when Sheelah was nigh,
No blithe Irish lad was so happy as I;
No harp like my own could so cheerily play,
And wherever I went was my poor dog Tray.

When at last I was forced from my Sheelah to part,
She said – while the sorrow was big at her heart –
"Oh! remember your Sheelah, when far, far away,
And be kind, my dear Pat, to our poor dog Tray."

Poor dog! he was faithful and kind, to be sure,
And he constantly loved me, although I was poor;
When the sour-looking folk sent me heartless away,
I had always a friend in my poor dog Tray.

When the road was so dark, and the night was so cold,
And Pat and his dog were grown weary and old,
How snugly we slept in my old coat of grey,
And he licked me for kindness – my poor dog Tray.

Though my wallet was scant, I remembered his case,
Nor refused my last crust to his pitiful face;
But he died at my feet on a cold winter day,
And I played a lament for my poor dog Tray.

Where now shall I go, forsaken and blind?
Can I find one to guide me, so faithful and kind?
To my sweet native village, so far, far away,
I can never return with my poor dog Tray.

THOMAS CAMPBELL

The Greater Cats

The greater cats with golden eyes
Stare out between the bars.
Deserts are there, and different skies,
And night with different stars.
They prowl the aromatic hill,
And mate as fiercely as they kill,
And hold the freedom of their will
To roam, to live, to drink their fill;
But this beyond their wit know I:
Man loves a little, and for long shall die.

Their kind across the desert range
Where tulips spring from stones,
Not knowing they will suffer change
Or vultures pick their bones.
Their strength's eternal in their sight,
They rule the terror of the night,
They overtake the deer in flight,
And in their arrogance they smite;
But I am sage, if they are strong:
Man's love is transient as his death is long.

Yet oh what powers to deceive!
My wit is turned to faith,
And at this moment I believe
In love, and scout at death.
I came from nowhere, and shall be
Strong, steadfast, swift, eternally:
I am a lion, a stone, a tree,
And as the Polar star in me
Is fixed my constant heart on thee.
Ah, may I stay forever blind
With lions, tigers, leopards, and their kind.

VITA SACKVILLE-WEST

The Tyger

Tyger! Tyger! burning bright
In the forests of the night,
What immortal hand or eye
Could frame thy fearful symmetry?

In what distant deeps or skies
Burnt the fire of thine eyes?
On what wings dare he aspire?
What the hand dare seize the fire?

And what shoulder, & what art,
Could twist the sinews of thy heart?
And when thy heart began to beat,
What dread hand? & what dread feet?

What the hammer? what the chain?
In what furnace was thy brain?
What the anvil? what dread grasp
Dare its deadly terrors clasp?

When the stars threw down their spears,
And water'd heaven with their tears,
Did he smile his work to see?
Did he who made the Lamb make thee?

Tyger! Tyger! burning bright
In the forests of the night,
What immortal hand or eye
Dare frame thy fearful symmetry?

WILLIAM BLAKE

The Fly

Little Fly,
Thy summer's play
My thoughtless hand
Has brush'd away.

Am not I
A fly like thee?
Or art not thou
A man like me?

For I dance,
And drink, & sing,
Till some blind hand
Shall brush my wing.

If thought is life
And strength & breath,
And the want
Of thought is death;

Then am I
A happy fly,
If I live
Or if I die.

WILLIAM BLAKE

On the Grasshopper and Cricket

The poetry of earth is never dead.
  When all the birds are faint with the hot sun
  And hide in cooling trees, a voice will run
From hedge to hedge about the new-mown mead –
That is the Grasshopper's. He takes the lead
  In summer luxury; he has never done
  With his delights, for when tired out with fun
He rests at ease beneath some pleasant weed.
The poetry of earth is ceasing never.
  On a lone winter evening, when the frost
    Has wrought a silence, from the stove there shrills
The cricket's song, in warmth increasing ever,
  And seems to one in drowsiness half lost,
    The grasshopper's among some grassy hills.

JOHN KEATS

The Song of Mr Toad

The world has held great Heroes,
  As history books have showed;
But never a name to go down to fame
  Compared with that of Toad!

The clever men at Oxford
  Know all that there is to be knowed,
But they none of them knew one half as much
  As intelligent Mr Toad!

The animals sat in the Ark and cried,
  Their tears in torrents flowed.
Who was it said, 'There's land ahead'?
  Encouraging Mr Toad!

The Army all saluted
  As they marched along the road.
Was it the King? Or Kitchener?
  No. It was Mr Toad!

The Queen and her Ladies-in-waiting
  Sat at the window and sewed.
She cried, 'Look! who's that *handsome* man?'
  They answered, 'Mr Toad.'

                    KENNETH GRAHAME

The Eagle

He clasps the crag with crooked hands;
Close to the sun in lonely lands,
Ring'd with the azure world, he stands.

The wrinkled sea beneath him crawls;
He watches from his mountain walls,
And like a thunderbolt he falls.

                    ALFRED, LORD TENNYSON

The Donkey

When fishes flew and forests walked
  And figs grew upon thorn,
Some moment when the moon was blood
  Then surely I was born.

With monstrous head and sickening cry
  And ears like errant wings,
The devil's walking parody
  On all four-footed things.

129

The tattered outlaw of the earth,
　Of ancient crooked will;
Starve, scourge, deride me: I am dumb,
　I keep my secret still.

Fools! For I also had my hour;
　One far fierce hour and sweet:
There was a shout about my ears,
　And palms before my feet.

G.K. CHESTERTON

The Toad beneath the Harrow

The toad beneath the harrow knows
Exactly where each tooth-point goes;
The butterfly upon the road
Preaches contentment to that toad.

RUDYARD KIPLING

Epigram

*Engraved on the collar of a dog which I gave to
His Royal Highness*
[Frederick, Prince of Wales, father of George III.]

I am his Highness' dog at Kew;
Pray tell me, sir, whose dog are you?

ALEXANDER POPE

Poor Old Horse

My clothing was once of the linsey woolsey fine,
My tail it grew at length, my coat did likewise shine;
But now I'm growing old; my beauty does decay,
My master frowns upon me; one day I heard him say,
Poor old horse: poor old horse.

Once I was kept in the stable snug and warm,
To keep my tender limbs from any cold or harm;
But now, in open fields, I am forced for to go,
In all sorts of weather, let it be hail, rain, freeze, or snow.
Poor old horse: poor old horse.

Once I was fed on the very best corn and hay
That ever grew in yon fields, or in yon meadows gay;
But now there's no such doing can I find at all,
I'm glad to pick the green sprouts that grow behind yon wall.
Poor old horse: poor old horse.

"You are old, you are cold, you are deaf, dull, dumb and slow,
You are not fit for anything, or in my team to draw.
You have eaten all my hay, you have spoiled all my straw,
So hang him, whip, stick him, to the huntsman let him go."
Poor old horse: poor old horse.

My hide unto the tanners then I would freely give,
My body to the hound dogs, I would rather die than live,
Likewise my poor old bones that have carried you many a mile,
Over hedges, ditches, brooks, bridges, likewise gates and stiles.
Poor old horse: poor old horse.

ANON

A Child's Pet

When I sailed out of Baltimore,
  With twice a thousand head of sheep,
They would not eat, they would not drink,
  But bleated o'er the deep.

131

Inside the pens we crawled each day,
  To sort the living from the dead;
And when we reached the Mersey's mouth,
  Had lost five hundred head.

Yet every night and day one sheep,
  That had no fear of man or sea,
Stuck through the bars its pleading face,
  And it was stroked by me.

And to the sheep-men standing near,
  'You see,' I said, 'this one tame sheep?
It seems a child has lost her pet,
  And cried herself to sleep.'

So every time we passed it by,
  Sailing to England's slaughter-house,
Eight ragged sheep-men – tramps and thieves –
  Would stroke that sheep's black nose.

W.H. DAVIES

Among all lovely things my Love had been

Among all lovely things my Love had been;
Had noted well the stars, all flowers that grew
About her home; but she had never seen
A Glow-worm, never one, and this I knew.

While riding near her home one stormy night
A single Glow-worm did I chance to espy;
I gave a fervent welcome to the sight,
And from my Horse I leapt; great joy had I.

Upon a leaf the Glow-worm did I lay,
To bear it with me through the stormy night:
And, as before, it shone without dismay;
Albeit putting forth a fainter light.

When to the Dwelling of my Love I came,
I went into the Orchard quietly;
And left the Glow-worm, blessing it by name,
Laid safely by itself, beneath a Tree.

The whole next day, I hoped, and hoped with fear;
At night the Glow-worm shone beneath the Tree:
I led my Lucy to the spot, 'Look here!'
Oh! joy it was for her, and joy for me!

WILLIAM WORDSWORTH

The Weasel

One morning a weasel came swimming
All the way over from France,
And taught all the weasels of England
To play on the fiddle and dance.

ANON

Epitaph on a Hare

Here lies, whom hound did ne'er pursue,
    Nor swifted greyhound follow,
Whose foot ne'er tainted morning dew,
    Nor ear heard huntsman's hallo',

Old Tiney, surliest of his kind,
    Who, nurs'd with tender care,
And to domestic bounds confin'd,
    Was still a wild Jack-hare.

Though duly from my hand he took
    His pittance ev'ry night,
He did it with a jealous look,
    And, when he could, would bite.

His diet was of wheaten bread,
  And milk, and oats, and straw,
Thistles, or lettuces instead,
  With sand to scour his maw.

On twigs of hawthorn he regal'd,
  On pippins' russet peel;
And, when his juicy salads fail'd,
  Slic'd carrot pleas'd him well.

A Turkey carpet was his lawn,
  Whereon he lov'd to bound,
To skip and gambol like a fawn,
  And swing his rump around.

His frisking was at evening hours,
  For then he lost his fear;
But most before approaching show'rs,
  Or when a storm drew near.

Eight years and five round rolling moons
  He thus saw steal away,
Dozing out all his idle noons,
  And ev'ry night at play.

I kept him for his humour's sake,
  For he would oft beguile
My heart of thoughts that made it ache,
  And force me to a smile.

But now, beneath this walnut-shade
  He finds his long, last home,
And waits in snug concealment laid,
  'Till gentler Puss shall come.

He, still more aged, feels the shocks
  From which no care can save,
And, partner once of Tiney's box,
  Must soon partake his grave.

WILLIAM COWPER

Plain Tales

Edward, Edward

Why does your brand so drop with blood,
    Edward, Edward?
Why does your brand so drop with blood?
    And why so sad go ye, oh?
Oh, I have killed my hawk so good,
    Mother, mother:
Oh, I have killed my hawk so good:
    And I had no more but he, oh.

Your hawkës blood was never so red,
    Edward, Edward;
Your hawkës blood was never so red,
    My dear son I tell thee, oh.
Oh, I have killed my red-roan steed,
    Mother, mother:
Oh, I have killed my red-roan steed
    That erst was so fair and free, oh.

Your steed was old, and ye have got more,
    Edward, Edward;
Your steed was old, and ye have got more;
    Some other dole ye dree, oh.
Oh, I have killed my father dear,
    Mother, mother:
Oh, I have killed my father dear,
    Alas and woe is me, oh.

And whatten penance will ye dree for that,
    Edward, Edward?
And whatten penance will ye dree for that?
    My dear son, now tell me, oh.
I'll set my feet in yonder boat,
    Mother, mother:
I'll set my feet in yonder boat,
    And I'll fare over the sea, oh.

And what will ye do with your towers and your hall,
    Edward, Edward?
And what will ye do with your towers and your hall
   That were so fair to see, oh?
I'll let them stand till they down fall,
    Mother, mother:
I'll let them stand till they down fall,
   For here never more maun I be, oh.

And what will ye leave to your bairns and your wife,
    Edward, Edward?
And what will ye leave to your bairns and your wife
   When ye go over the sea, oh?
The worldës room, let them beg through life,
    Mother, mother:
The worldës room, let them beg through life,
   For them never more will I see, oh.

And what will ye leave to your own mother dear,
    Edward, Edward?
And what will ye leave to your own mother dear?
   My dear son, now tell me, oh.
The curse of hell from me shall ye bear,
    Mother, mother:
The curse of hell from me shall ye bear,
   Such counsels ye gave to me, oh.

ANON

The War-Song of Dinas Vawr

The mountain sheep are sweeter,
But the valley sheep are fatter;
We therefore deemed it meeter
To carry off the latter.
We made an expedition;
We met a host, and quelled it;
We forced a strong position,
And killed the men who held it.

136

On Dyfed's richest valley,
Where herds of kine were brousing,
We made a mighty sally,
To furnish our carousing.
Fierce warriors rushed to meet us;
We met them, and o'erthrew them:
They struggled hard to beat us;
But we conquered them, and slew them.

As we drove our prize at leisure,
The king marched forth to catch us:
His rage surpassed all measure,
But his people could not match us.
He fled to his hall-pillars;
And, ere our force we led off,
Some sacked his house and cellars,
While others cut his head off.

We there, in strife bewild'ring,
Spilt blood enough to swim in:
We orphaned many children,
And widowed many women.
The eagles and the ravens
We glutted with our foemen;
The heroes and the cravens,
The spearmen and the bowmen.

We brought away from battle,
And much their land bemoaned them,
Two thousand head of cattle,
And the head of him who owned them:
Ednyfed, king of Dyfed,
His head was borne before us;
His wine and beasts supplied our feasts,
And his overthrow, our chorus.

THOMAS LOVE PEACOCK

The Court Historian

Lower Empire. Circa A.D. 700

The Monk Arnulphus uncork'd his ink
  That shone with a blood-red light
Just now as the sun began to sink;
  His vellum was pumiced a silvery white;
'The Basileus' – for so he began –
  'Is a royal sagacious Mars of a man,
    Than the very lion bolder;
He has married the stately widow of Thrace –'
  'Hush!' cried a voice at his shoulder.

His palette gleam'd with a burnish'd green,
  Bright as a dragon-fly's skin:
His gold-leaf shone like the robe of a queen,
  His azure glow'd as a cloud worn thin,
Deep as the blue of the king-whale's lair:
  'The Porphyrogenita Zoë the fair
    Is about to wed with a Prince much older,
Of an unpropitious mien and look –'
  'Hush!' cried a voice at his shoulder.

The red flowers trellis'd the parchment page,
  The birds leap'd up on the spray,
The yellow fruit sway'd and droop'd and swung,
  It was Autumn mixt up with May.
(O, but his cheek was shrivell'd and shrunk!)
'The child of the Basileus,' wrote the Monk,
  'Is golden-hair'd – tender the Queen's arms fold her.
Her step-mother Zoë doth love her so –'
  'Hush!' cried a voice at his shoulder.

The Kings and Martyrs and Saints and Priests
  All gather'd to guard the text:
There was Daniel snug in the lions' den
  Singing no whit perplex'd –
Brazen Samson with spear and helm –
'The Queen,' wrote the Monk, 'rules firm this realm,
  For the King gets older and older.
The Norseman Thorkill is brave and fair –'
  'Hush!' cried a voice at his shoulder.

WALTER THORNBURY

The Eve of St Agnes

I

St Agnes' Eve – ah, bitter chill it was!
The owl, for all his feathers, was a-cold;
The hare limped trembling through the frozen grass,
And silent was the flock in woolly fold.
Numb were the Beadsman's fingers, while he told
His rosary, and while his frosted breath,
Like pious incense from a censer old,
Seemed taking flight for heaven, without a death,
Past the sweet Virgin's picture, while his prayer he saith.

II

His prayer he saith, this patient, holy man;
Then takes his lamp, and riseth from his knees,
And back returneth, meagre, barefoot, wan,
Along the chapel aisle by slow degrees.
The sculptured dead, on each side, seem to freeze,
Imprisoned in black, purgatorial rails.
Knights, ladies, praying in dumb orat'ries,
He passeth by; and his weak spirit fails
To think how they may ache in icy hoods and mails.

III

Northward he turneth through a little door,
And scarce three steps, ere music's golden tongue
Flattered to tears this agèd man and poor;
But no – already had his deathbell rung,
The joys of all his life were said and sung;
His was harsh penance on St Agnes' Eve.
Another way he went, and soon among
Rough ashes sat he for his soul's reprieve,
And all night kept awake for sinners' sake to grieve.

IV

That ancient Beadsman heard the prelude soft,
And so it chanced for many a door was wide
From hurry to and fro. Soon, up aloft,
The silver, snarling trumpets 'gan to chide;
The level chambers, ready with their pride,
Were glowing to receive a thousand guests;
The carvèd angels, ever eager-eyed,
Stared, where upon their heads the cornice rests,
With hair blown back, and wings put cross-wise on their breasts.

139

V

At length burst in the argent revelry,
With plume, tiara, and all rich array,
Numerous as shadows haunting fairily
The brain, new stuffed in youth, with triumphs gay
Of old romance. These let us wish away,
And turn, sole-thoughted, to one Lady there,
Whose heart had brooded, all that wintry day,
On love, and winged St Agnes' saintly care,
As she had heard old dames full many times declare.

VI

They told her how, upon St Agnes' Eve,
Young virgins might have visions of delight,
And soft adorings from their loves receive
Upon the honeyed middle of the night,
If ceremonies due they did aright;
As, supperless to bed they must retire,
And couch supine their beauties, lily white,
Nor look behind, nor sideways, but require
Of Heaven with upward eyes for all that they desire.

VII

Full of this whim was thoughtful Madeline.
The music, yearning like a God in pain,
She scarcely heard; her maiden eyes divine,
Fixed on the floor, saw many a sweeping train
Pass by – she heeded not at all; in vain
Came many a tiptoe, amorous cavalier,
And back retired – not cooled by high disdain,
But she saw not; her heart was otherwhere.
She sighed for Agnes' dreams, the sweetest of the year.

VIII

She danced along with vague, regardless eyes,
Anxious her lips, her breathing quick and short.
The hallowed hour was near at hand. She sighs
Amid the timbrels and the thronged resort
Of whisperers in anger, or in sport;
'Mid looks of love, defiance, hate, and scorn,
Hoodwinked with fairy fancy – all amort,
Save to St Agnes and her lambs unshorn,
And all the bliss to be before to-morrow morn.

IX

So, purposing each moment to retire,
She lingered still. Meantime, across the moors,
Had come young Porphyro, with heart on fire
For Madeline. Beside the portal doors,
Buttressed from moonlight, stands he and implores
All saints to give him sight of Madeline
But for one moment in the tedious hours,
That he might gaze and worship all unseen;
Perchance speak, kneel, touch, kiss – in sooth such things have
    been.

X

He ventures in – let no buzzed whisper tell,
All eyes be muffled, or a hundred swords
Will storm his heart, love's feverous citadel.
For him, those chambers held barbarian hordes,
Hyena foemen, and hot-blooded lords,
Whose very dogs would execrations howl
Against his lineage; not one breast affords
Him any mercy, in that mansion foul,
Save one old beldame, weak in body and in soul.

XI

Ah, happy chance! The agèd creature came,
Shuffling along with ivory-headed wand,
To where he stood, hid from the torch's flame,
Behind a broad hall-pillar, far beyond
The sound of merriment and chorus bland.
He startled her; but soon she knew his face,
And grasped his fingers in her palsied hand,
Saying, 'Mercy, Porphyro! Hie thee from this place;
They are all here to-night, the whole blood-thirsty race!

XII

Get hence! Get hence! There's dwarfish Hildebrand –
He had a fever late, and in the fit
He cursèd thee and thine, both house and land;
Then there's that old Lord Maurice, not a whit
More tame for his gray hairs. Alas me! Flit,
Flit like a ghost away!' 'Ah, gossip dear,
We're safe enough; here in this arm-chair sit,
And tell me how –' 'Good Saints! Not here, not here;
Follow me, child, or else these stones will be thy bier.'

XIII

He followed through a lowly archèd way,
Brushing the cobwebs with his lofty plume,
And as she muttered, 'Well-a – well-a-day!'
He found him in a little moonlight room,
Pale, latticed, chill, and silent as a tomb.
'Now tell me where is Madeline,' said he,
'Oh, tell me, Angela, by the holy loom
Which none but secret sisterhood may see,
When they St Agnes' wool are weaving piously.'

XIV

'St Agnes? Ah! It is St Agnes' Eve –
Yet men will murder upon holy days:
Thou must hold water in a witch's sieve,
And be liege-lord of all the elves and fays,
To venture so; it fills me with amaze
To see thee, Porphyro! – St Agnes' Eve!
God's help! My lady fair the conjuror plays
This very night. Good angels her deceive!
But let me laugh awhile, I've mickle time to grieve.'

XV

Feeble she laugheth in the languid moon,
While Porphyro upon her face doth look,
Like puzzled urchin on an agèd crone
Who keepeth closed a wondrous riddle-book,
As spectacled she sits in chimney nook.
But soon his eyes grew brilliant, when she told
His lady's purpose, and he scarce could brook
Tears at the thought of those enchantments cold,
And Madeline asleep in lap of legends old.

XVI

Sudden a thought came like a full-blown rose,
Flushing his brow, and in his painèd heart
Made purple riot; then doth he propose
A stratagem that makes the beldame start:
'A cruel man and impious thou art –
Sweet lady, let her pray, and sleep, and dream
Alone with her good angels, far apart
From wicked men like thee. Go, go! I deem
Thou canst not surely be the same that thou didst seem.'

XVII

'I will not harm her, by all saints I swear,'
Quoth Porphyro: 'Oh, may I ne'er find grace
When my weak voice shall whisper its last prayer,
If one of her soft ringlets I displace,
Or look with ruffian passion in her face –
Good Angela, believe me by these tears,
Or I will, even in a moment's space,
Awake with horrid shout my foemen's ears,
And beard them, though they be more fanged than wolves and
    bears.'

XVIII

'Ah, why wilt thou affright a feeble soul?
A poor, weak, palsy-stricken, churchyard thing,
Whose passing-bell may ere the midnight toll!
Whose prayers for thee, each morn and evening,
Were never missed.' Thus plaining doth she bring
A gentler speech from burning Porphyro,
So woeful, and of such deep sorrowing,
That Angela gives promise she will do
Whatever he shall wish, betide her weal or woe.

Which was to lead him, in close secrecy,
Even to Madeline's chamber, and there hide
Him in a closet, of such privacy
That he might see her beauty unespied,
And win perhaps that night a peerless bride,
While legioned fairies paced the coverlet
And pale enchantment held her sleepy-eyed.
Never on such a night have lovers met
Since Merlin paid his Demon all the monstrous debt.

XX

'It shall be as thou wishest,' said the Dame,
'All cates and dainties shall be storèd there
Quickly on this feast-night; by the tambour frame
Her own lute thou wilt see. No time to spare,
For I am slow and feeble, and scarce dare
On such a catering trust my dizzy head.
Wait here, my child, with patience; kneel in prayer
The while. Ah! Thou must needs the lady wed,
Or may I never leave my grave among the dead.'

XXI

So saying, she hobbled off with busy fear.
The lover's endless minutes slowly passed;
The dame returned, and whispered in his ear
To follow her; with agèd eyes aghast
From fright of dim espial. Safe at last,
Through many a dusky gallery, they gain
The maiden's chamber, silken, hushed, and chaste,
Where Porphyro took covert, pleased amain.
His poor guide hurried back with agues in her brain.

XXII

Her faltering hand upon the balustrade,
Old Angela was feeling for the stair,
When Madeline, St Agnes' charmèd maid,
Rose, like a missioned spirit, unaware.
With silver taper's light, and pious care,
She turned, and down the agèd gossip led
To a safe level matting. Now prepare,
Young Porphyro, for gazing on that bed –
She comes, she comes again, like ring-dove frayed and fled.

XXIII

Out went the taper as she hurried in;
Its little smoke, in pallid moonshine, died.
She closed the door, she panted, all akin
To spirits of the air, and visions wide –
No uttered syllable, or woe betide!
But to her heart, her heart was voluble,
Paining with eloquence her balmy side,
As though a tongueless nightingale should swell
Her throat in vain, and die, heart-stifled, in her dell.

XXIV

A casement high and triple-arched there was,
All garlanded with carven imageries
Of fruits, and flowers, and bunches of knot-grass,
And diamonded with panes of quaint device
Innumerable of stains and splendid dyes,
As are the tiger-moth's deep-damasked wings;
And in the midst, 'mong thousand heraldries,
And twilight saints, and dim emblazonings,
A shielded scutcheon blushed with blood of queens and kings.

XXV

Full on this casement shone the wintry moon,
And threw warm gules on Madeline's fair breast
As down she knelt for heaven's grace and boon;
Rose-bloom fell on her hands, together pressed,
And on her silver cross soft amethyst,
And on her hair a glory, like a saint.
She seemed a splendid angel, newly dressed,
Save wings, for Heaven. Porphyro grew faint;
She knelt, so pure a thing, so free from mortal taint.

XXVI

Anon his heart revives; her vespers done,
Of all its wreathèd pearls her hair she frees;
Unclasps her warmèd jewels one by one;
Loosens her fragrant bodice; by degrees
Her rich attire creeps rustling to her knees.
Half-hidden, like a mermaid in sea-weed,
Pensive awhile she dreams awake, and sees,
In fancy, fair St Agnes in her bed,
But dares not look behind, or all the charm is fled.

XXVII

Soon, trembling in her soft and chilly nest,
In sort of wakeful swoon, perplexed she lay,
Until the poppied warmth of sleep oppressed
Her soothèd limbs, and soul fatigued – away
Flown, like a thought, until the morrow-day;
Blissfully havened both from joy and pain;
Clasped like a missal where swart Paynims pray;
Blinded alike from sunshine and from rain,
As though a rose should shut, and be a bud again.

XXVIII

Stol'n to this paradise, and so entranced,
Porphyro gazed upon her empty dress,
And listened to her breathing, if it chanced
To wake into a slumbrous tenderness;
Which when he heard, that minute did he bless,
And breathed himself, then from the closet crept,
Noiseless as fear in a wide wilderness –
And over the hushed carpet, silent, stepped,
And 'tween the curtains peeped, where, lo! – how fast she slept.

XXIX

Then by the bed-side, where the faded moon
Made a dim, silver twilight, soft he set
A table and, half anguished, threw thereon
A cloth of woven crimson, gold, and jet.
Oh, for some drowsy Morphean amulet!
The boisterous, midnight, festive clarion,
The kettle-drum and far-heard clarionet,
Affray his ears, though but in dying tone;
The hall door shuts again, and all the noise is gone.

XXX

And still she slept an azure-lidded sleep,
In blanchèd linen, smooth and lavendered,
While he from forth the closet brought a heap
Of candied apple, quince, and plum, and gourd,
With jellies soother than the creamy curd,
And lucent syrops, tinct with cinnamon;
Manna and dates, in argosy transferred
From Fez; and spicèd dainties, every one,
From silken Samarcand to cedared Lebanon.

XXXI

These delicates he heaped with glowing hand
On golden dishes and in baskets bright
Of wreathèd silver; sumptuous they stand
In the retired quiet of the night,
Filling the chilly room with perfume light.
'And now, my love, my seraph fair, awake!
Thou art my heaven, and I thine eremite.
Open thine eyes, for meek St Agnes' sake,
Or I shall drowse beside thee, so my soul doth ache.'

XXXII

Thus whispering, his warm, unnervèd arm
Sank in her pillow. Shaded was her dream
By the dusk curtains; 'twas a midnight charm
Impossible to melt as icèd stream.
The lustrous salvers in the moonlight gleam,
Broad golden fringe upon the carpet lies.
It seemed he never, never could redeem
From such a steadfast spell his lady's eyes;
So mused awhile, entoiled in woofèd phantasies.

XXXIII

Awakening up, he took her hollow lute,
Tumultuous, and, in chords that tenderest be,
He played an ancient ditty, long since mute,
In Provence called, 'La belle dame sans mercy',
Close to her ear touching the melody –
Wherewith disturbed, she uttered a soft moan.
He ceased – she panted quick – and suddenly
Her blue affrayèd eyes wide open shone;
Upon his knees he sank, pale as smooth-sculptured stone.

XXXIV

Her eyes were open, but she still beheld,
Now wide awake, the vision of her sleep –
There was a painful change, that nigh expelled
The blisses of her dream so pure and deep.
At which fair Madeline began to weep,
And moan forth witless words with many a sigh,
While still her gaze on Porphyro would keep;
Who knelt, with joinèd hands and piteous eye,
Fearing to move or speak, she looked so dreamingly.

XXXV

'Ah, Porphyro!' said she, 'but even now
Thy voice was at sweet tremble in mine ear,
Made tuneable with every sweetest vow,
And those sad eyes were spiritual and clear.
How changed thou art! How pallid, chill, and drear!
Give me that voice again, my Porphyro,
Those looks immortal, those complainings dear!
Oh, leave me not in this eternal woe,
For if thou diest, my love, I know not where to go.'

XXXVI

Beyond a mortal man impassioned far
At these voluptuous accents, he arose,
Ethereal, flushed, and like a throbbing star
Seen mid the sapphire heaven's deep repose;
Into her dream he melted, as the rose
Blendeth its odour with the violet,
Solution sweet – meantime the frost-wind blows
Like Love's alarum pattering the sharp sleet
Against the window-panes; St Agnes' moon hath set.

XXXVII

'Tis dark; quick pattereth the flaw-blown sleet.
'This is no dream, my bride, my Madeline!'
'Tis dark; the icèd gusts still rave and beat.
'No dream, alas! alas! and woe is mine!
Porphyro will leave me here to fade and pine.
Cruel! What traitor could thee hither bring?
I curse not, for my heart is lost in thine,
Though thou forsakest a deceivèd thing –
A dove forlorn and lost with sick, unprunèd wing.'

XXXVIII

'My Madeline! Sweet dreamer! Lovely bride!
Say, may I be for ay thy vassal blest?
Thy beauty's shield, heart-shaped and vermeil dyed?
Ah, silver shrine, here will I take my rest
After so many hours of toil and quest,
A famished pilgrim – saved by miracle.
Though I have found, I will not rob thy nest
Saving of thy sweet self; if thou think'st well
To trust, fair Madeline, to no rude infidel.

Hark! 'Tis an elfin-storm from fairy land,
Of haggard seeming, but a boon indeed.
Arise – arise! The morning is at hand;
The bloated wassailers will never heed.
Let us away, my love, with happy speed –
There are no ears to hear, or eyes to see,
Drowned all in Rhenish and the sleepy mead.
Awake! Arise, my love, and fearless be!
For o'er the southern moors I have a home for thee.'

She hurried at his words, beset with fears,
For there were sleeping dragons all around,
At glaring watch, perhaps, with ready spears;
Down the wide stairs a darkling way they found.
In all the house was heard no human sound;
A chain-drooped lamp was flickering by each door;
The arras, rich with horseman, hawk, and hound,
Fluttered in the besieging wind's uproar;
And the long carpets rose along the gusty floor.

They glide, like phantoms, into the wide hall;
Like phantoms, to the iron porch they glide;
Where lay the Porter, in uneasy sprawl,
With a huge empty flagon by his side.
The wakeful bloodhound rose and shook his hide,
But his sagacious eye an inmate owns.
By one, and one, the bolts full easy slide;
The chains lie silent on the footworn stones;
The key turns, and the door upon its hinges groans.

XLII

And they are gone – aye, ages long ago
These lovers fled away into the storm.
That night the Baron dreamt of many a woe,
And all his warrior-guests, with shade and form
Of witch and demon, and large coffin-worm,
Were long be-nightmared. Angela the old
Died palsy-twitched, with meagre face deform;
The Beadsman, after thousand aves told,
For ay unsought for slept among his ashes cold.

JOHN KEATS

Mazeppa's Ride

I

'Twas after dread Pultowa's day,
    When Fortune left the royal Swede –
Around a slaughtered army lay,
    No more to combat and to bleed.
The power and glory of the war,
    Faithless as their vain votaries, men,
Had passed to the triumphant Czar,
    And Moscow's walls were safe again –
Until a day more dark and drear
And a more memorable year,
Should give to slaughter and to shame
A mightier host and haughtier name;
A greater wreck, a deeper fall,
A shock to one – a thunderbolt to all.

149

II

Such was the hazard of the die;
The wounded Charles was taught to fly
By day and night through field and flood,
Stained with his own and subjects' blood;
For thousands fell that flight to aid:
And not a voice was heard to upbraid
Ambition in his humbled hour,
When Truth had nought to dread from Power.
His horse was slain, and Gieta gave
His own – and died the Russians' slave.
This, too, sinks after many a league
Of well-sustained, but vain fatigue;
And in the depth of forests darkling,
The watch-fires in the distance sparkling –
    The beacons of surrounding foes –
A King must lay his limbs at length.
    Are these the laurels and repose
For which the nations strain their strength?
They laid him by a savage tree,
In outworn Nature's agony;
His wounds were stiff, his limbs were stark;
The heavy hour was chill and dark;
The fever in his blood forbade
A transient slumber's fitful aid:
And thus it was; but yet through all,
Kinglike the Monarch bore his fall,
And made, in this extreme of ill,
His pangs the vassals of his will:
All silent and subdued were they,
As once the nations round him lay. [...]

VIII

"For lovers there are many eyes,
    And such there were on us; the Devil
    On such occasions should be civil –
The Devil! – I'm loth to do him wrong,
    It might be some untoward saint,
Who would not be at rest too long,
    But to his pious bile gave vent –
But one fair night, some lurking spies
Surprised and seized us both.
The Count was something more than wroth –
I was unarmed; but if in steel,

All cap-à-pie from head to heel,
What 'gainst their numbers could I do?
'Twas near his castle, far away
   From city or from succour near,
And almost on the break of day;
I did not think to see another,
   My moments seemed reduced to few;
And with one prayer to Mary Mother,
   And, it may be, a saint or two,
As I resigned me to my fate,
They led me to the castle gate:
   Theresa's doom I never knew,
Our lot was henceforth separate. –
An angry man, ye may opine,
Was he, the proud Count Palatine;
And he had reason good to be,
   But he was most enraged lest such
   An accident should chance to touch
Upon his future pedigree;
Nor less amazed, that such a blot
His noble 'scutcheon should have got,
While he was highest of his line;
   Because unto himself he seemed
   The first of men, nor less he deemed
In others' eyes, and most in mine.
'Sdeath! with a *page* – perchance a king
Had reconciled him to the thing;
But with a stripling of a page –
I felt – but cannot paint his rage.

IX

" 'Bring forth the horse!' – the horse was brought!
In truth, he was a noble steed,
   A Tartar of the Ukraine breed,
Who looked as though the speed of thought
Were in his limbs; but he was wild,
   Wild as the wild deer, and untaught,
With spur and bridle undefiled –
   'Twas but a day he had been caught;
And snorting, with erected mane,
And struggling fiercely, but in vain
In the full foam of wrath and dread
To me the desert-born was led:
They bound me on, that menial throng,

151

Upon his back with many a thong;
They loosed him with a sudden lash –
Away! – away! – and on we dash! –
Torrents less rapid and less rash.

X

"Away! – away! – My breath was gone,
I saw not where he hurried on:
'Twas scarcely yet the break of day,
And on he foamed – away! – away!
The last of human sounds which rose,
As I was darted from my foes,
Was the wild shout of savage laughter,
Which on the wind came roaring after
A moment from that rabble rout:
With sudden wrath I wrenched my head,
   And snapped the cord, which to the mane
   Had bound my neck in lieu of rein,
And, writhing half my form about,
Howled back my curse; but 'midst the tread,
The thunder of my courser's speed,
Perchance they did not hear nor heed:
It vexes me – for I would fain
Have paid their insult back again.
I paid it well in after days:
There is not of that castle gate,
Its drawbridge and portcullis' weight,
Stone – bar – moat – bridge – or barrier left;
Nor of its fields a blade of grass,
   Save what grows on a ridge of wall,
   Where stood the hearth-stone of the hall;
And many a time ye there might pass,
Nor dream that e'er the fortress was.
I saw its turrets in a blaze,
Their crackling battlements all cleft,
   And the hot lead pour down like rain
From off the scorched and blackening roof
Whose thickness was not vengeance-proof.
   They little thought that day of pain,
When launched, as on the lightning's flash,
They bade me to destruction dash,
   That one day I should come again,
With twice five thousand horse, to thank
   The Count for his uncourteous ride.

They played me then a bitter prank,
   When, with the wild horse for my guide,
They bound me to his foaming flank:
At length I played them one as frank –
For Time at last sets all things even –
   And if we do but watch the hour,
   There never yet was human power
Which could evade, if unforgiven,
The patient search and vigil long
Of him who treasures up a wrong.

XI

"Away! – away! – my steed and I,
   Upon the pinions of the wind!
   All human dwellings left behind,
We sped like meteors through the sky,
When with its crackling sound the night
Is chequered with the Northern light.
Town – village – none were on our track,
   But a wild plain of far extent,
And bounded by a forest black;
   And, save the scarce seen battlement
On distant heights of some strong hold,
Against the Tartars built of old,
No trace of man. The year before
A Turkish army had marched o'er;
And where the Spahi's hoof hath trod,
The verdure flies the bloody sod:
The sky was dull, and dim, and gray,
   And a low breeze crept moaning by –
   I could have answered with a sigh –
But fast we fled, – away! – away! –
And I could neither sigh nor pray;
And my cold sweat-drops fell like rain
Upon the courser's bristling mane;
But, snorting still with rage and fear,
He flew upon his far career:
At times I almost thought, indeed,
He must have slackened in his speed;
But no – my bound and slender frame
   Was nothing to his angry might,
And merely like a spur became:
Each motion which I made to free
My swoln limbs from their agony

153

Increased his fury and affright:
I tried my voice, – 'twas faint and low –
But yet he swerved as from a blow;
And, starting to each accent, sprang
As from a sudden trumpet's clang:
Meantime my cords were wet with gore,
Which, oozing through my limbs, ran o'er;
And in my tongue the thirst became
A something fiercer far than flame.

XII

"We neared the wild wood – 'twas so wide,
I saw no bounds on either side:
'Twas studded with old sturdy trees,
That bent not to the roughest breeze
Which howls down from Siberia's waste,
And strips the forest in its haste, –
But these were few and far between,
Set thick with shrubs more young and green,
Luxuriant with their annual leaves,
Ere strown by those autumnal eves
That nip the forest's foliage dead,
Discoloured with a lifeless red,
Which stands thereon like stiffened gore
Upon the slain when battle's o'er;
And some long winter's night hath shed
Its frost o'er every tombless head –
So cold and stark – the raven's beak
May peck unpierced each frozen cheek:
'Twas a wild waste of underwood,
And here and there a chestnut stood,
The strong oak, and the hardy pine;
  But far apart – and well it were,
Or else a different lot were mine –
  The boughs gave way, and did not tear
My limbs; and I found strength to bear
My wounds, already scarred with cold;
My bonds forbade to loose my hold.
We rustled through the leaves like wind, –
Left shrubs, and trees, and wolves behind;
By night I heard them on the track,
Their troop came hard upon our back,
With their long gallop, which can tire
The hound's deep hate, and hunter's fire:

154

Where'er we flew they followed on,
Nor left us with the morning sun;
Behind I saw them, scarce a rood,
At day-break winding through the wood,
And through the night had heard their feet
Their stealing, rustling step repeat.
Oh! how I wished for spear or sword,
At least to die amidst the horde,
And perish – if it must be so –
At bay, destroying many a foe!
When first my courser's race begun,
I wished the goal already won;
But now I doubted strength and speed:
Vain doubt! his swift and savage breed
Had nerved him like the mountain-roe –
Nor faster falls the blinding snow
Which whelms the peasant near the door
Whose threshold he shall cross no more,
Bewildered with the dazzling blast,
Than through the forest-paths he passed –
Untired, untamed, and worse than wild –
All furious as a favoured child
Balked of its wish; or – fiercer still –
A woman piqued – who has her will!

XIII

"The wood was passed; 'twas more than noon,
But chill the air, although in June;
Or it might be my veins ran cold –
Prolonged endurance tames the bold;
And I was then not what I seem,
But headlong as a wintry stream,
And wore my feelings out before
I well could count their causes o'er:
And what with fury, fear, and wrath,
The tortures which beset my path –
Cold – hunger – sorrow – shame – distress –
Thus bound in Nature's nakedness;
Sprung from a race whose rising blood
When stirred beyond its calmer mood,
And trodden hard upon, is like
The rattle-snake's, in act to strike –
What marvel if this worn-out trunk
Beneath its woes a moment sunk?

The earth gave way, the skies rolled round,
I seemed to sink upon the ground;
But erred – for I was fastly bound.
My heart turned sick, my brain grew sore,
And throbbed awhile, then beat no more:
The skies spun like a mighty wheel;
I saw the trees like drunkards reel,
And a slight flash sprang o'er my eyes,
Which saw no farther. He who dies
Can die no more than then I died,
O'ertortured by that ghastly ride.
I felt the blackness come and go,
    And strove to wake; but could not make
My senses climb up from below:
I felt as on a plank at sea,
When all the waves that dash o'er thee,
At the same time upheave and whelm,
And hurl thee towards a desert realm.
My undulating life was as
The fancied lights that flitting pass
Our shut eyes in deep midnight, when
Fever begins upon the brain;
But soon it passed, with little pain,
    But a confusion worse than such:
    I own that I should deem it much,
Dying, to feel the same again;
And yet I do suppose we must
Feel far more e'er we turn to dust!
No matter! I have bared my brow
Full in Death's face – before – and now.

XIV

"My thoughts came back. Where was I? Cold,
    And numb, and giddy: pulse by pulse
Life reassumed its lingering hold,
And throb by throb, – till grown a pang
    Which for a moment could convulse,
    My blood reflowed, though thick and chill;
My ear with uncouth noises rang,
    My heart began once more to thrill;
My sight returned, though dim; alas!
And thickened, as it were, with glass.
Methought the dash of waves was nigh;
There was a gleam too of the sky,

156

Studded with stars; – it is no dream;
The wild horse swims the wilder stream!
The bright broad river's gushing tide
Sweeps, winding onward, far and wide,
And we are half-way, struggling o'er
To yon unknown and silent shore.
The waters broke my hollow trance,
And with a temporary strength
   My stiffened limbs were rebaptized.
My courser's broad breast proudly braves,
And dashes off the ascending waves,
And onward we advance!
We reach the slippery shore at length,
   A haven I but little prized,
For all behind was dark and drear,
And all before was night and fear.
How many hours of night or day
In those suspended pangs I lay,
I could not tell; I scarcely knew
If this were human breath I drew.

XV

"With glossy skin, and dripping mane,
   And reeling limbs, and reeking flank,
The wild steed's sinewy nerves still strain
   Up the repelling bank.
We gain the top: a boundless plain
Spreads through the shadow of the night,
   And onward, onward, onward – seems,
   Like precipices in our dreams,
To stretch beyond the sight;
And here and there a speck of white,
   Or scattered spot of dusky green,
In masses broke into the light,
As rose the moon upon my right:
   But nought distinctly seen
In the dim waste would indicate
The omen of a cottage gate;
No twinkling taper from afar
Stood like a hospitable star;
Not even an ignis-fatuus rose
To make him merry with my woes:
   That very cheat had cheered me then!
Although detected, welcome still,

157

Reminding me, through every ill,
  Of the abodes of men.

XVI

"Onward we went – but slack and slow;
  His savage force at length o'erspent,
The drooping courser, faint and low,
  All feebly foaming went:
A sickly infant had had power
To guide him forward in that hour!
  But, useless all to me,
His new-born tameness nought availed –
My limbs were bound; my force had failed,
  Perchance, had they been free.
With feeble effort still I tried
To rend the bonds so starkly tied,
  But still it was in vain;
My limbs were only wrung the more,
And soon the idle strife gave o'er,
  Which but prolonged their pain.
The dizzy race seemed almost done,
Although no goal was nearly won:
Some streaks announced the coming sun –
  How slow, alas! he came!
Methought that mist of dawning gray
Would never dapple into day,
How heavily it rolled away!
  Before the eastern flame
Rose crimson, and deposed the stars,
And called the radiance from their cars,
And filled the earth, from his deep throne,
With lonely lustre, all his own.

XVII

"Uprose the sun; the mists were curled
Back from the solitary world
Which lay around – behind – before.
What booted it to traverse o'er
Plain – forest – river? Man nor brute,
Nor dint of hoof, nor print of foot,
Lay in the wild luxuriant soil –
No sign of travel, none of toil –
The very air was mute:
And not an insect's shrill small horn,

158

Nor matin bird's new voice was borne
From herb nor thicket. Many a *werst*,
Panting as if his heart would burst,
The weary brute still staggered on;
And still we were – or seemed – alone:
At length, while reeling on our way,
Methought I heard a courser neigh,
From out yon tuft of blackening firs.
Is it the wind those branches stirs?
No, no! From out the forest prance
   A trampling troop; I see them come!
In one vast squadron they advance!
   I strove to cry – my lips were dumb!
The steeds rush on in plunging pride;
But where are they the reins to guide?
A thousand horse, and none to ride!
With flowing tail, and flying mane,
Wide nostrils never stretched by pain,
Mouths bloodless to the bit or rein,
And feet that iron never shod,
And flanks unscarred by spur or rod,
A thousand horse, the wild, the free,
Like waves that follow o'er the sea,
    Came thickly thundering on,
As if our faint approach to meet!
The sight re-nerved my courser's feet,
A moment staggering, feebly fleet,
A moment, with a faint low neigh,
   He answered, and then fell!
With gasps and glazing eyes he lay,
   And reeking limbs immoveable,
    His first and last career is done!
On came the troop – they saw him stoop,
   They saw me strangely bound along
   His back with many a bloody thong.
They stop – they start – they snuff the air,
Gallop a moment here and there,
Approach, retire, wheel round and round,
Then plunging back with sudden bound,
Headed by one black mighty steed,
Who seemed the Patriarch of his breed,
   Without a single speck or hair
Of white upon his shaggy hide;
They snort – they foam – neigh – they swerve aside,

And backward to the forest fly,
By instinct, from a human eye.
　They left me there to my despair,
Linked to the dead and stiffening wretch,
Whose lifeless limbs beneath me stretch,
Relieved of that unwonted weight,
From whence I could not extricate
Nor him nor me – and there we lay,
　The dying on the dead!
I little deemed another day
　Would see my houseless, helpless head.

"And there from morn to twilight bound,
I felt the heavy hours toil round,
With just enough of life to see
My last of suns go down on me,
In hopeless certainty of mind,
That makes us feel at length resigned
To that which our foreboding years
Present the worst and last of fears:
Inevitable – even a boon,
Nor more unkind for coming soon,
Yet shunned and dreaded with such care,
As if it only were a snare
　That Prudence might escape:
At times both wished for and implored,
At times sought with self-pointed sword,
Yet still a dark and hideous close
To even intolerable woes,
　And welcome in no shape.
And, strange to say, the sons of pleasure,
They who have revelled beyond measure
In beauty, wassail, wine, and treasure,
Die calm, or calmer, oft than he
Whose heritage was Misery:
For he who hath in turn run through
All that was beautiful and new,
　Hath nought to hope, and nought to leave;
And, save the future, (which is viewed
Not quite as men are base and good,
But as their nerves may be endued,)
　With nought perhaps to grieve:
The wretch still hopes his woes must end,
And Death, whom he should deem his friend,

Appears, to his distempered eyes,
Arrived to rob him of his prize,
The tree of his new Paradise.
To-morrow would have given him all,
Repaid his pangs, repaired his fall;
To-morrow would have been the first
Of days no more deplored or curst,
But bright, and long, and beckoning years,
Seen dazzling through the mist of tears,
Guerdon of many a painful hour;
To-morrow would have given him power
To rule – to shine – to smite – to save –
And must it dawn upon his grave?

XVIII

"The sun was sinking – still I lay
    Chained to the chill and stiffening steed!
I thought to mingle there our clay;
    And my dim eyes of death had need,
    No hope arose of being freed.
I cast my last looks up the sky,
    And there between me and the sun
I saw the expecting raven fly,
Who scarce would wait till both should die,
    Ere his repast begun;
He flew, and perched, then flew once more,
And each time nearer than before;
I saw his wing through twilight flit,
And once so near me he alit
    I could have smote, but lacked the strength;
But the slight motion of my hand,
And feeble scratching of the sand,
The exerted throat's faint struggling noise,
Which scarcely could be called a voice,
    Together scared him off at length.
I know no more – my latest dream
    Is something of a lovely star
    Which fixed my dull eyes from afar,
And went and came with wandering beam,
And of the cold – dull – swimming – dense
Sensation of recurring sense,
And then subsiding back to death,
And then again a little breath,
A little thrill – a short suspense,

161

An icy sickness curdling o'er
My heart, and sparks that crossed my brain –
A gasp – a throb – a start of pain,
A sigh – and nothing more...."

GEORGE GORDON, LORD BYRON

Incident of the French Camp

You know, we French stormed Ratisbon:
    A mile or so away,
On a little mound, Napoleon
    Stood on our storming-day;
With neck out-thrust, you fancy how,
    Legs wide, arms locked behind,
As if to balance the prone brow
    Oppressive with its mind.

Just as perhaps he mused 'My plans
    'That soar, to earth may fall,
'Let once my army-leader Lannes
    'Waver at yonder wall,' –
Out 'twixt the battery-smokes there flew
    A rider, bound on bound
Full-galloping; nor bridle drew
    Until he reached the mound.

Then off there flung in smiling joy,
    And held himself erect
By just his horse's mane, a boy:
    You hardly could suspect –
(So tight he kept his lips compressed,
    Scarce any blood came through)
You looked twice ere you saw his breast
    Was all but shot in two.

'Well,' cried he, 'Emperor, by God's grace
    'We've got you Ratisbon!
'The Marshal's in the market-place,
    'And you'll be there anon

162

'To see your flag-bird flap his vans
    'Where I, to heart's desire,
'Perched him!' The chief's eye flashed; his plans
    Soared up again like fire.

The chief's eye flashed; but presently
    Softened itself, as sheathes
A film the mother-eagle's eye
    When her bruised eaglet breathes;
'You're wounded!' 'Nay,' the soldier's pride
    Touched to the quick, he said:
'I'm killed, Sire!' And his chief beside
    Smiling the boy fell dead.

                    ROBERT BROWNING

Lepanto

White founts falling in the courts of the sun,
And the Soldan of Byzantium is smiling as they run;
There is laughter like the fountains in that face of all men feared,
It stirs the forest darkness, the darkness of his beard,
It curls the blood-red crescent, the crescent of his lips,
For the inmost sea of all the earth is shaken with his ships.
They have dared the white republics up the capes of Italy,
They have dashed the Adriatic round the Lion of the Sea,
And the Pope has cast his arms abroad for agony and loss,
And called the kings of Christendom for swords about the Cross,
The cold queen of England is looking in the glass;
The shadow of the Valois is yawning at the Mass;
From evening isles fantastical rings faint the Spanish gun,
And the Lord upon the Golden Horn is laughing in the sun.

Dim drums throbbing, in the hills half heard,
Where only on a nameless throne a crownless prince has stirred,
Where, risen from a doubtful seat and half-attainted stall,
The last knight of Europe takes weapons from the wall,
The last and lingering troubadour to whom the bird had sung,
That once went singing southward when all the world was young,
In that enormous silence, tiny and unafraid,
Comes up along a winding road the noise of the Crusade.

Strong gongs groaning as the guns boom far,
Don John of Austria is going to the war,
Stiff flags straining in the night-blasts cold
In the gloom black-purple, in the glint old-gold,
Torchlight crimson on the copper kettle-drums,
Then the tuckets, then the trumpets, then the cannon, and he
    comes.
Don John laughing in the brave beard curled,
Spurning of his stirrups like the thrones of all the world,
Holding his head up for a flag of all the free.
Love-light of Spain – hurrah!
Death-light of Africa!
Don John of Austria
Is riding to the sea.

Mahound is in his paradise above the evening star,
(Don John of Austria is going to the war.)
He moves a mighty turban on the timeless houri's knees,
His turban that is woven of the sunset and the seas.
He shakes the peacock gardens as he rises from his ease,
And he strides among the tree-tops and is taller than the trees,
And his voice through all the garden is a thunder sent to bring
Black Azrael and Ariel and Ammon on the wing.
Giants and the Genii,
Multiplex of wing and eye,
Whose strong obedience broke the sky
When Solomon was king.

They rush in red and purple from the red clouds of the morn,
From temples where the yellow gods shut up their eyes in scorn;
They rise in green robes roaring from the green hells of the sea
Where fallen skies and evil hues and eyeless creatures be;
On them the sea-valves cluster and the grey sea-forests curl,
Splashed with a splendid sickness, the sickness of the pearl;
They swell in sapphire smoke out of the blue cracks of the ground, –
They gather and they wonder and give worship to Mahound.
And he saith, "Break up the mountains where the hermit-folk
    may hide,
And sift the red and silver sands lest bone of saint abide,
And chase the Giaours flying night and day, not giving rest,
For that which was our trouble comes again out of the west.
We have set the seal of Solomon on all things under sun,
Of knowledge and of sorrow and endurance of things done,
But a noise is in the mountains, in the mountains, and I know

164

The voice that shook our palaces – four hundred years ago:
It is he that saith not 'Kismet'; it is he that knows not Fate;
It is Richard, it is Raymond, it is Godfrey in the gate!
It is he whose loss is laughter when he counts the wager worth,
Put down your feet upon him, that our peace be on the earth."
For he heard drums groaning and he heard guns jar,
(Don John of Austria is going to the war.)
Sudden and still – hurrah!
Bolt from Iberia!
Don John of Austria
Is gone by Alcalar.

St. Michael's on his Mountain in the sea-roads of the north
(Don John of Austria is girt and going forth.)
Where the grey seas glitter and the sharp tides shift
And the sea folk labour and the red sails lift.
He shakes his lance of iron and he claps his wings of stone;
The noise is gone through Normandy; the noise is gone alone;
The North is full of tangled things and texts and aching eyes
And dead is all the innocence of anger and surprise,
And Christian killeth Christian in a narrow dusty room,
And Christian dreadeth Christ that hath a newer face of doom,
And Christian hateth Mary that God kissed in Galilee,
But Don John of Austria is riding to the sea.
Don John calling through the blast and the eclipse
Crying with the trumpet, with the trumpet of his lips,
Trumpet that sayeth ha!
    Domino gloria!
Don John of Austria
Is shouting to the ships.
King Philip's in his closet with the Fleece about his neck
(Don John of Austria is armed upon the deck.)
The walls are hung with velvet that is black and soft as sin,
And little dwarfs creep out of it and little dwarfs creep in.
He holds a crystal phial that has colours like the moon,
He touches, and it tingles, and he trembles very soon,
And his face is as a fungus of a leprous white and grey
Like plants in the high houses that are shuttered from the day,
And death is in the phial, and the end of noble work,
But Don John of Austria has fired upon the Turk.
Don John's hunting, and his hounds have bayed –
Booms away past Italy the rumour of his raid.
Gun upon gun, ha! ha!
Gun upon gun, hurrah!

Don John of Austria
Has loosed the cannonade.

The Pope was in his chapel before day or battle broke,
(Don John of Austria is hidden in the smoke.)
The hidden room in a man's house where God sits all the year,
The secret window whence the world looks small and very dear.
He sees as in a mirror on the monstrous twilight sea
The crescent of his cruel ships whose name is mystery;
They fling great shadows foe-wards, making Cross and Castle dark,
They veil the plumèd lions on the galleys of St Mark;
And above the ships are palaces of brown, black-bearded chiefs,
And below the ships are prisons, where with multitudinous griefs,
Christian captives sick and sunless, all a labouring race repines
Like a race in sunken cities, like a nation in the mines.
They are lost like slaves that swat, and in the skies of morning
        hung
The stairways of the tallest gods when tyranny was young.
They are countless, voiceless, hopeless as those fallen or fleeing on
Before the high Kings' horses in the granite of Babylon.
And many a one grows witless in his quiet room in hell
Where a yellow face looks inward through the lattice of his cell,
And he finds his God forgotten, and he seeks no more a sign –
(But Don John of Austria has burst the battle-line!)
Don John pounding from the slaughter-painted poop,
Purpling all the ocean like a bloody pirate's sloop,
Scarlet running over on the silvers and the golds,
Breaking of the hatches up and bursting of the holds,
Thronging of the thousands up that labour under sea
White for bliss and blind for sun and stunned for liberty.
Vivat Hispania!
Domino Gloria!
Don John of Austria
Has set his people free!

Cervantes on his galley sets the sword back in the sheath
(Don John of Austria rides homeward with a wreath.)
And he sees across a weary land a straggling road in Spain,
Up which a lean and foolish knight forever rides in vain,
And he smiles, but not as Sultans smile, and settles back the
        blade...
(But Don John of Austria rides home from the Crusade.)

                                                    G.K. CHESTERTON

The Armada

Attend, all ye who list to hear our noble England's praise;
I tell of the thrice famous deeds she wrought in ancient days,
When that great fleet invincible against her bore in vain
The richest spoils of Mexico, the stoutest hearts of Spain.
　It was about the lovely close of a warm summer day,
There came a gallant merchant-ship full sail to Plymouth Bay;
Her crew hath seen Castile's black fleet, beyond Aurigny's isle,
At earliest twilight, on the waves lie heaving many a mile.
At sunrise she escaped their van, by God's especial grace;
And the tall Pinta, till the noon, had held her close in chase.
Forthwith a guard at every gun was placed along the wall;
The beacon blazed upon the roof of Edgecumbe's lofty hall;
Many a light fishing-bark put out to pry along the coast,
And with loose rein and bloody spur rode inland many a post.
With his white hair unbonneted, the stout old sheriff comes;
Behind him march the halberdiers; before him sound the drums;
His yeomen round the market cross make clear an ample space;
For there behoves him to set up the standard of Her Grace.
And haughtily the trumpets peal, and gaily dance the bells,
As slow upon the labouring wind the royal blazon swells.
Look how the Lion of the sea lifts up his ancient crown,
And underneath his deadly paw treads the gay lilies down.
So stalked he when he turned to flight, on that famed Picard field,
Bohemia's plume, and Genoa's bow, and Cæsar's eagle shield.
So glared he when at Agincourt in wrath he turned to bay,
And crushed and torn beneath his claws the princely hunters lay.
Ho! strike the flagstaff deep, sir Knight: ho! scatter flowers fair
　　maids:
Ho! gunners, fire a loud salute: ho! gallants, draw your blades:
Thou sun, shine on her joyously; ye breezes, waft her wide;
Our glorious SEMPER EADEM, the banner of our pride.
　The freshening breeze of eve unfurled that banner's massy fold;
The parting gleam of sunshine kissed that haughty scroll of gold;
Night sank upon the dusky beach, and on the purple sea,
Such night in England ne'er had been, nor e'er again shall be.
From Eddystone to Berwick bounds, from Lynn to Milford Bay,
That time of slumber was as bright and busy as the day;
For swift to east and swift to west the ghastly war-flame spread,
High on St Michael's Mount it shone: it shone on Beachy Head.
Far on the deep the Spaniard saw, along each southern shire,
Cape beyond cape, in endless range, those twinkling points of
　　fire.

167

The fisher left his skiff to rock on Tamar's glittering waves:
The rugged miners poured to war from Mendip's sunless caves:
O'er Longleat's towers, o'er Cranbourne's oaks, the fiery herald
flew:
He roused the shepherds of Stonehenge, the rangers of Beaulieu.
Right sharp and quick the bells all night rang out from Bristol town,
And ere the day three hundred horse had met on Clifton down;
The sentinel on Whitehall gate looked forth into the night,
And saw o'erhanging Richmond Hill the streak of blood-red light.
Then bugle's note and cannon's roar the deathlike silence broke,
And with one start, and with one cry, the royal city woke.
At once on all her stately gates arose the answering fires;
At once the wild alarum clashed from all her reeling spires;
From all the batteries of the Tower pealed loud the voice of fear;
And all the thousand masts of Thames sent back a louder cheer:
And from the furthest wards was heard the rush of hurrying feet,
And the broad streams of pikes and flags rushed down each
roaring street;
And broader still became the blaze, and louder still the din,
As fast from every village round the horse came spurring in:
And eastward straight from wild Blackheath the warlike errand
went,
And roused in many an ancient hall the gallant squires of Kent.
Southward from Surrey's pleasant hills flew those bright couriers
forth;
High on bleak Hampstead's swarthy moor they started for the
north;
And on, and on, without a pause, untired they bounded still:
All night from tower to tower they sprang; they sprang from hill
to hill:
Till the proud peak unfurled the flag o'er Darwin's rocky dales,
Till like volcanoes flared to heaven the stormy hills of Wales,
Till twelve fair counties saw the blaze on Malvern's lonely height,
Till streamed in crimson on the wind the Wrekin's crest of light,
Till broad and fierce the star came forth on Ely's stately fane,
And tower and hamlet rose in arms o'er all the boundless plain;
Till Belvoir's lordly terraces the sign to Lincoln sent,
And Lincoln sped the message on o'er the wide vale of Trent;
Till Skiddaw saw the fire that burned on Gaunt's embattled pile,
And the red glare on Skiddaw roused the burghers of Carlisle.

THOMAS BABINGTON MACAULAY

The Forsaken Merman

Come, dear children, let us away;
    Down and away below.
Now my brothers call from the bay;
Now the great winds shorewards blow;
Now the salt tides seawards flow;
Now the wild white horses play,
Champ and chafe and toss in the spray.
    Children dear, let us away.
        This way, this way.

Call her once before you go –
    Call once yet!
In a voice that she will know:
    "Margaret! Margaret!"
Children's voices should be dear
(Call once more) to a mother's ear:
Children's voices, wild with pain –
    Surely she will come again!
Call her once and come away;
        This way, this way!
"Mother dear, we cannot stay."
The wild white horses foam and fret
        Margaret! Margaret!

Come, dear children, come away down;
    Call no more!
One last look at the white-wall'd town,
And the little grey church on the windy shore;
    Then come down!
She will not come though you call all day;
    Come away, come away!

Children dear, was it yesterday
We heard the sweet bells over the bay?
    In the caverns where we lay,
    Through the surf and through the swell,
The far-off sound of a silver bell?
Sand-strewn caverns, cool and deep,
Where the winds are all asleep;
Where the spent lights quiver and gleam;
Where the salt weed sways in the stream;
Where the sea-beasts, ranged all round,

Feed in the ooze of their pasture-ground;
Where the sea-snakes coil and twine,
Dry their mail and bask in the brine;
Where great whales come sailing by,
Sail and sail, with unshut eye,
Round the world for ever and aye?
  When did music come this way?
  Children dear, was it yesterday?

  Children dear, was it yesterday
  (Call yet once) that she went away?
  Once she sate with you and me,
  On a red gold throne in the heart of the sea,
  And the youngest sate on her knee.
She comb'd its bright hair, and she tended it well,
When down swung the sound of a far-off bell.
She sigh'd, she look'd up through the clear green sea.
She said; "I must go, for my kinsfolk pray
In the little grey church on the shore to-day.
'Twill be Easter-time in the world – ah me!
And I lose my poor soul, Merman, here with thee."
I said; "Go up, dear heart, through the waves.
Say thy prayer, and come back to the kind sea-caves."
  She smiled, she went up through the surf in the bay.
  Children dear, was it yesterday?

  Children dear, were we long alone?
"The sea grows stormy, the little ones moan;
Long prayers," I said, "in the world they say;
Come," I said, and we rose through the surf in the bay.
We went up the beach, by the sandy down
Where the sea-stocks bloom, to the white-wall'd town.
Through the narrow paved streets, where all was still,
To the little grey church on the windy hill.
From the church came a murmur of folk at their prayers,
But we stood without in the cold blowing airs.
We climb'd on the graves, on the stones worn with rains,
And we gazed up the aisle through the small leaded panes.
  She sate by the pillar; we saw her clear:
  "Margaret, hist! come quick, we are here.
  Dear heart," I said, "we are long alone;
  The sea grows stormy, the little ones moan."
But, ah, she gave me never a look,
For her eyes were seal'd to the holy book!

Loud prays the priest; shut stands the door.
Come away, children, call no more.
Come away, come down, call no more.

Down, down, down!
Down to the depths of the sea!
She sits at her wheel in the humming town,
    Singing most joyfully.
Hark, what she sings; "O joy, O joy,
For the humming street, and the child with its toy!
For the priest, and the bell, and the holy well.
    For the wheel where I spun,
    And the blessed light of the sun!"
And so she sings her fill,
Singing most joyfully,
Till the spindle falls from her hand,
And the whizzing wheel stands still.
She steals to the window, and looks at the sand;
    And over the sand at the sea;
    And her eyes are set in a stare;
    And anon there breaks a sigh,
    And anon there drops a tear,
    From a sorrow-clouded eye,
    And a heart sorrow-laden,
        A long, long sigh.
For the cold strange eyes of a little Mermaiden,
    And the gleam of her golden hair.

Come away, away children.
Come children, come down.
The hoarse wind blows coldly;
Lights shine in the town.
She will start from her slumber
When gusts shake the door;
She will hear the winds howling,
Will hear the waves roar.
We shall see, while above us
The waves roar and whirl,
A ceiling of amber,
A pavement of pearl.
Singing, "Here came a mortal,
But faithless was she!
And alone dwell for ever
The kings of the sea."

171

But, children, at midnight,
When soft the winds blow;
When clear falls the moonlight;
When spring-tides are low:
When sweet airs come seaward
From heaths starr'd with broom;
And high rocks throw mildly
On the blanch'd sands a gloom:
Up the still, glistening beaches,
Up the creeks we will hie;
Over banks of bright seaweed
The ebb-tide leaves dry.
We will gaze, from the sand-hills,
At the white, sleeping town;
At the church on the hill-side –
    And then come back down.
Singing, "There dwells a loved one,
But cruel is she!
She left lonely for ever
The kings of the sea."

MATTHEW ARNOLD

The Changeling

Toll no bell for me, dear Father, dear Mother,
    Waste no sighs;
There are my sisters, there is my little brother
    Who plays in the place called Paradise,
Your children all, your children for ever;
        But I, so wild,
Your disgrace, with the queer brown face, was never,
    Never, I know, but half your child!

In the garden at play, all day, last summer,
        Far and away I heard
The sweet "tweet-tweet" of a strange new-comer,
    The dearest, clearest call of a bird.
It lived down there in the deep green hollow,
    My own old home, and the fairies say
The word of a bird is a thing to follow,
    So I was away a night and a day.

172

One evening, too, by the nursery fire,
　　We snuggled close and sat round so still,
When suddenly as the wind blew higher,
　　Something scratched on the window-sill.
A pinched brown face peered in – I shivered;
　　No one listened or seemed to see;
The arms of it waved and the wings of it quivered,
　　Whoo – I knew it had come for me;
　　Some are as bad as bad can be!
All night long they danced in the rain,
Round and round in a dripping chain,
Threw their caps at the window-pane,
　　Tried to make me scream and shout
　　And fling the bedclothes all about:
I meant to stay in bed that night,
And if only you had left a light
　　They would never have got me out.

　　Sometimes I wouldn't speak, you see,
　　Or answer when you spoke to me,
Because in the long, still dusks of Spring
You can hear the whole world whispering;
　　The shy green grasses making love,
　　The feathers grow on the dear, grey dove,
　　The tiny heart of the redstart beat,
　　The patter of the squirrel's feet,
The pebbles pushing in the silver streams,
The rushes talking in their dreams,
　　The swish-swish of the bat's black wings,
　　The wild-wood bluebell's sweet ting-tings,
　　　Humming and hammering at your ear,
　　　Everything there is to hear
In the heart of hidden things,
　　But not in the midst of the nursery riot,
　　That's why I wanted to be quiet,
　　　Couldn't do my sums, or sing,
　　　Or settle down to anything.
　　And when, for that, I was sent upstairs
　　I *did* kneel down to say my prayers;
But the King who sits on your high church steeple
Has nothing to do with us fairy people!

'Times I pleased you, dear Father, dear Mother,
　　Learned all my lessons and liked to play,

173

And dearly I loved the little pale brother
  Whom some other bird must have called away.
Why did They bring me here to make me
  Not quite bad and not quite good,
Why, unless They're wicked, do They want, in spite, to take me
  Back to their wet, wild wood?
Now, every night I shall see the windows shining,
  The gold lamp's glow, and the fire's red gleam,
While the best of us are twining twigs and the rest of us are whining
   In the hollow by the stream.
Black and chill are Their nights on the wold;
  And They live so long and They feel no pain:
I shall grow up, but never grow old,
I shall always, always be very cold,
   I shall never come back again!

CHARLOTTE MEW

The Craftsman

Once, after long-drawn revel at The Mermaid,
He to the overbearing Boanerges
Jonson, uttered (if half of it were liquor,
    Blessed be the vintage!)

Saying how, at an alehouse under Cotswold,
He had made sure of his very Cleopatra
Drunk with enormous, salvation-contemning
    Love for a tinker.

How, while he hid from Sir Thomas's keepers,
Crouched in a ditch and drenched by the midnight
Dews, he had listened to gipsy Juliet
    Rail at the dawning.

How at Bankside, a boy drowning kittens
Winced at the business; whereupon his sister –
Lady Macbeth aged seven – thrust 'em under,
    Sombrely scornful.

How on a Sabbath, hushed and compassionate –
She being known since her birth to the townsfolk –
Stratford dredged and delivered from Avon
            Dripping Ophelia.

So, with a thin third finger marrying
Drop to wine-drop domed on the table,
Shakespeare opened his heart till the sunrise
            Entered to hear him.

London waked and he, imperturbable,
Passed from waking to hurry after shadows.
Busied upon shows of no earthly importance?
            Yes, but he knew it!

                     RUDYARD KIPLING

Sir Patrick Spens

The king sits in Dunfermlin town
   Drinking the blood-red wine:
Oh where will I get a good sailor
   To sail this ship of mine?

Up and spake an eldern knight
   Sat at the king's right knee:
Sir Patrick Spens is the best sailor
   That sails upon the sea.

The king has written a broad letter
   And signed it with his hand,
And sent it to Sir Patrick Spens
   Was walking on the strand.

To Noroway, to Noroway,
   To Noroway o'er the foam,
The king's daughter to Noroway,
   'Tis thou maun bring her home.

The first line that Sir Patrick read
   A loud laugh laughed he;

The next line that Sir Patrick read
 A tear blinded his eye.

Oh who is this has done this deed,
 This ill deed done to me,
To send me out this time of the year
 To sail upon the sea?

Make haste, make haste, my merry men all;
 Our good ship sails the morn.
Oh say not so, my master dear,
 For I fear a deadly storm.

Late, late yestreen I saw the new moon
 With the old moon in her arm,
And I fear, I fear, my master dear,
 That we will come to harm.

They hadna sailed a league, a league,
 A league but barely three,
When the air grew dark, and the wind blew loud,
 And growly grew the sea.

Oh our Scotch nobles were right loth
 To wet their cork-heeled shoon,
But long ere all the play were played
 Their hats they swam aboon.

Oh long, long may their ladies sit
 With their fans into their hand
Ere ever they see Sir Patrick Spens
 Come sailing to the land.

Oh long, long may the ladies stand
 With their gold combs in their hair
Waiting for their own dear lords,
 For they'll see them no more.

Half o'er, half o'er to Aberdour
 It's fifty fathom deep,
And there lies good Sir Patrick Spens
 With the Scotch lords at his feet.

ANON

Horatius

Lars Porsena of Clusium
  By the Nine Gods he swore
That the great house of Tarquin
  Should suffer wrong no more.
By the Nine Gods he swore it,
  And named a trysting day,
And bade his messengers ride forth,
East and west and south and north,
  To summon his array.

East and west and south and north
  The messengers ride fast,
And tower and town and cottage
  Have heard the trumpet's blast.
Shame on the false Etruscan
  Who lingers in his home,
When Porsena of Clusium
  Is on the march for Rome.

The horsemen and the footmen
  Are pouring in amain
From many a stately market-place;
  From many a fruitful plain;
From many a lonely hamlet,
  Which, hid by beech and pine,
Like an eagle's nest, hangs on the crest
  Of purple Apennine;

From lordly Volaterræ,
  Where scowls the far-famed hold
Piled by the hands of giants
  For godlike kings of old;
From seagirt Populonia,
  Whose sentinels descry
Sardinia's snowy mountain-tops
  Fringing the southern sky;

From the proud mart of Pisæ,
  Queen of the western waves,
Where ride Massilia's triremes
  Heavy with fair-haired slaves;

177

From where sweet Clanis wanders
    Through corn and vines and flowers;
From where Cortona lifts to heaven
    Her diadem of towers.

Tall are the oaks whose acorns
    Drop in dark Auser's rill;
Fat are the stags that champ the boughs
    Of the Ciminian hill;
Beyond all streams Clitumnus
    Is to the herdsman dear;
Best of all pools the fowler loves
    The great Volsinian mere.

But now no stroke of woodman
    Is heard by Auser's rill;
No hunter tracks the stag's green path
    Up the Ciminian hill;
Unwatched along Clitumnus
    Grazes the milk-white steer;
Unharmed the water fowl may dip
    In the Volsinian mere.

The harvests of Arretium,
    This year, old men shall reap;
This year, young boys in Umbro
    Shall plunge the struggling sheep;
And in the vats of Luna,
    This year, the must shall foam
Round the white feet of laughing girls
    Whose sires have marched to Rome.

There be thirty chosen prophets,
    The wisest of the land,
Who alway by Lars Porsena
    Both morn and evening stand:
Evening and morn the Thirty
    Have turned the verses o'er,
Traced from the right on linen white
    By mighty seers of yore.

And with one voice the Thirty
    Have their glad answer given:
'Go forth, go forth, Lars Porsena;
    Go forth, beloved of Heaven;

Go, and return in glory
  To Clusium's royal dome;
And hang round Nurscia's altars
  The golden shields of Rome.'

And now hath every city
  Sent up her tale of men;
The foot are fourscore thousand,
  The horse are thousands ten.
Before the gates of Sutrium
  Is met the great array.
A proud man was Lars Porsena
  Upon the trysting day.

For all the Etruscan armies
  Were ranged beneath his eye,
And many a banished Roman,
  And many a stout ally;
And with a mighty following
  To join the muster came
The Tusculan Mamilius,
  Prince of the Latian name.

But by the yellow Tiber
  Was tumult and affright:
From all the spacious champaign
  To Rome men took their flight.
A mile around the city,
  The throng stopped up the ways:
A fearful sight it was to see
  Through two long nights and days

For aged folks on crutches,
  And women great with child,
And mothers sobbing over babes
  That clung to them and smiled.
And sick men borne in litters
  High on the necks of slaves,
And troops of sun-burned husbandmen
  With reaping-hooks and staves,

And droves of mules and asses
  Laden with skins of wine,
And endless flocks of goats and sheep,
  And endless herds of kine,

179

And endless trains of waggons
  That creaked beneath the weight
Of corn-sacks and of household goods,
  Choked every roaring gate.

Now, from the rock Tarpeian,
  Could the wan burghers spy
The line of blazing villages
  Red in the midnight sky.
The Fathers of the City,
  They sat all night and day,
For every hour some horseman came
  With tidings of dismay.

To eastward and to westward
  Have spread the Tuscan bands;
Nor house, nor fence, nor dovecote
  In Crustumerium stands.
Verbenna down to Ostia
  Hath wasted all the plain;
Astur hath stormed Janiculum,
  And the stout guards are slain.

I wis, in all the Senate,
  There was no heart so bold,
But sore it ached, and fast it beat,
  When that ill news was told.
Forthwith up rose the Consul,
  Up rose the Fathers all;
In haste they girded up their gowns,
  And hied them to the wall.

They held a council standing
  Before the River-Gate;
Short time was there, ye well may guess,
  For musing or debate.
Out spake the Consul roundly:
  'The bridge must straight go down;
For, since Janiculum is lost,
  Nought else can save the town.'

Just then a scout came flying,
  All wild with haste and fear:
'To arms! to arms! Sir Consul:
  Lars Porsena is here.'

On the low hills to westward
  The Consul fixed his eye,
And saw the swarthy storm of dust
  Rise fast along the sky.

And nearer fast and nearer
  Doth the red whirlwind come;
And louder still and still more loud,
From underneath that rolling cloud,
Is heard the trumpet's war-note proud
  The trampling, and the hum.
And plainly and more plainly
  Now through the gloom appears,
Far to left and far to right.
In broken gleams of dark-blue light,
The long array of helmets bright,
  The long array of spears.

And plainly and more plainly,
  Above that glimmering line,
Now might ye see the banners
  Of twelve fair cities shine;
But the banner of proud Clusium
  Was highest of them all,
The terror of the Umbrian,
  The terror of the Gaul.

And plainly and more plainly
  Now might the burghers know,
By port and vest, by horse and crest,
  Each warlike Lucumo.
There Cilnius of Arretium
  On his fleet roan was seen;
And Astur of the four-fold shield,
Girt with the brand none else may wield,
Tolumnius with the belt of gold,
And dark Verbenna from the hold
  By reedy Thrasymene.

Fast by the royal standard,
  O'erlooking all the war,
Lars Porsena of Clusium
  Sat in his ivory car.

By the right wheel rode Mamilius,
    Prince of the Latian name;
And by the left false Sextus,
    That wrought the deed of shame.

But when the face of Sextus
    Was seen among the foes,
A yell that rent the firmament
    From all the town arose.
On the house-tops was no woman
    But spat towards him and hissed
No child but screamed out curses,
    And shook its little fist.

But the Consul's brow was sad,
    And the Consul's speech was low,
And darkly looked he at the wall,
    And darkly at the foe.
'Their van will be upon us
    Before the bridge goes down;
And if they once may win the bridge,
    What hope to save the town?'

Then out spake brave Horatius,
    The Captain of the Gate:
'To every man upon this earth
    Death cometh soon or late.
And how can man die better
    Than facing fearful odds,
For the ashes of his fathers,
    And the temples of his Gods,

'And for the tender mother
    Who dandled him to rest,
And for the wife who nurses
    His baby at her breast,
And for the holy maidens
    Who feed the eternal flame,
To save them from false Sextus
    That wrought the deed of shame?

'Hew down the bridge, Sir Consul,
    With all the speed ye may;
I, with two more to help me,
    Will hold the foe in play.

In yon strait path a thousand
  May well be stopped by three.
Now who will stand on either hand,
  And keep the bridge with me?'

Then out spake Spurius Lartius;
  A Ramnian proud was he:
'Lo, I will stand at thy right hand,
  And keep the bridge with thee.'
And out spake strong Herminius;
  Of Titian blood was he:
'I will abide on thy left side,
  And keep the bridge with thee.'

'Horatius,' quoth the Consul,
  'As thou sayest, so let it be.'
And straight against that great array
  Forth went the dauntless Three.
For Romans in Rome's quarrel
  Spared neither land nor gold,
Nor son nor wife, nor limb nor life,
  In the brave days of old.

Then none was for a party;
  Then all were for the state;
Then the great man helped the poor,
  And the poor man loved the great.
Then lands were fairly portioned;
  Then spoils were fairly sold:
The Romans were like brothers
  In the brave days of old.

Now Roman is to Roman
  More hateful than a foe,
And the Tribunes beard the high,
  And the Fathers grind the low.
As we wax hot in faction,
  In battle we wax cold:
Wherefore men fight not as they fought
  In the brave days of old.

Now while the Three were tightening
  Their harness on their backs,
The Consul was the foremost man
  To take in hand an axe:

And Fathers mixed with Commons
  Seized hatchet, bar, and crow,
And smote upon the planks above,
  And loosed the props below.

Meanwhile the Tuscan army,
  Right glorious to behold,
Came flashing back the noonday light,
Rank behind rank, like surges bright
  Of a broad sea of gold.
Four hundred trumpets sounded
  A peal of warlike glee,
As that great host, with measured tread,
And spears advanced, and ensigns spread,
Rolled slowly towards the bridge's head,
  Where stood the dauntless Three.

The Three stood calm and silent,
  And looked upon the foes,
And a great shout of laughter
  From all the vanguard rose:
And forth three chiefs came spurring
  Before that deep array;
To earth they sprang, their swords they drew,
And lifted high their shields, and flew
  To win the narrow way;

Aunus from green Tifernum,
  Lord of the Hill of Vines;
And Seius, whose eight hundred slaves
  Sicken in Ilva's mines;
And Picus, long to Clusium
  Vassal in peace and war,
Who led to fight his Umbrian powers
From that grey crag where, girt with towers,
The fortress of Nequinum lowers
  O'er the pale waves of Nar.

Stout Lartius hurled down Aunus
  Into the stream beneath:
Herminius struck at Seius,
  And clove him to the teeth:
At Picus brave Horatius
  Darted one fiery thrust;

184

And the proud Umbrian's gilded arms
    Clashed in the bloody dust.

Then Ocnus of Falerii
    Rushed on the Roman Three;
And Lausulus of Urgo,
    The rover of the sea;
And Aruns of Volsinium,
    Who slew the great wild boar,
The great wild boar that had his den
Amidst the reeds of Cosa's fen,
And wasted fields, and slaughtered men,
    Along Albinia's shore.

Herminius smote down Aruns:
    Lartius laid Ocnus low:
Right to the heart of Lausulus
    Horatius sent a blow.
'Lie there,' he cried, 'fell pirate!
    No more, aghast and pale,
From Ostia's walls the crowd shall mark
The track of thy destroying bark.
No more Campania's hinds shall fly
To woods and caverns when they spy
    Thy thrice accursed sail.'

But now no sound of laughter
    Was heard among the foes.
A wild and wrathful clamour
    From all the vanguard rose.
Six spears' lengths from the entrance
    Halted that deep array,
And for a space no man came forth
    To win the narrow way.

But hark! the cry is Astur:
    And lo! the ranks divide;
And the great Lord of Luna
    Comes with his stately stride.
Upon his ample shoulders
    Clangs loud the four-fold shield,
And in his hand he shakes the brand
    Which none but he can wield.

He smiled on those bold Romans
   A smile serene and high;
He eyed the flinching Tuscans,
   And scorn was in his eye.
Quoth he, 'The she-wolf's litter
   Stand savagely at bay:
But will ye dare to follow,
   If Astur clears the way?'

Then, whirling up his broadsword
   With both hands to the height,
He rushed against Horatius,
   And smote with all his might.
With shield and blade Horatius
   Right deftly turned the blow.
The blow, though turned, came yet too nigh;
It missed his helm, but gashed his thigh:
The Tuscans raised a joyful cry
   To see the red blood flow.

He reeled, and on Herminius
   He leaned one breathing-space;
Then, like a wild cat mad with wounds,
   Sprang right at Astur's face.
Through teeth, and skull, and helmet
   So fierce a thrust he sped,
The good sword stood a hand-breadth out
   Behind the Tuscan's head.

And the great Lord of Luna
   Fell at that deadly stroke,
As falls on Mount Alvernus
   A thunder-smitted oak.
Far o'er the crashing forest
   The giant arms lie spread;
And the pale augurs, muttering low,
   Gaze on the blasted head.

On Astur's throat Horatius
   Right firmly pressed his heel,
And thrice and four times tugged amain,
   Ere he wrenched out the steel.
'And see,' he cried, 'the welcome,
   Fair guests, that waits you here!

What noble Locumo comes next
　　To taste our Roman cheer?'

But at his haughty challenge
　　A sullen murmur ran,
Mingled of wrath, and shame, and dread,
　　Along that glittering van.
There lacked not men of prowess,
　　Nor men of lordly race;
For all Etruria's noblest
　　Were round the fatal place.

But all Etruria's noblest
　　Felt their hearts sink to see
On the earth the bloody corpses,
　　In the path the dauntless Three;
And, from the ghastly entrance
　　Where those bold Romans stood,
All shrank, like boys who unaware,
Ranging the woods to start a hare,
Come to the mouth of a dark lair
Where, growling low, a fierce old bear
　　Lies amidst bones and blood.

Was none who would be foremost
　　To lead such dire attack:
But those behind cried 'Forward!'
　　And those before cried 'Back!'
And backward now and forward
　　Wavers the deep array;
And on the tossing sea of steel,
To and fro the standards reel;
And the victorious trumpet-peal
　　Dies fitfully away.

Yet one man for one moment
　　Strode out before the crowd;
Well known was he to all the Three,
　　And they gave him greeting loud.
'Now welcome, welcome, Sextus!
　　Now welcome to thy home!
Why dost thou stay, and turn away?
　　Here lies the road to Rome.'

Thrice looked he at the city;
　Thrice looked he at the dead;
And thrice came on in fury,
　And thrice turned back in dread:
And, white with fear and hatred,
　Scowled at the narrow way
Where, wallowing in a pool of blood,
　The bravest Tuscans lay.

But meanwhile axe and lever
　Have manfully been plied;
And now the bridge hangs tottering
　Above the boiling tide.
'Come back, come back, Horatius!'
　Loud cried the Fathers all.
'Back, Lartius! back, Herminius!
　Back, ere the ruin fall!'

Back darted Spurius Lartius;
　Herminius darted back:
And, as they passed, beneath their feet
　They felt the timbers crack.
But when they turned their faces,
　And on the farther shore
Saw brave Horatius stand alone,
　They would have crossed once more.

But with a crash like thunder
　Fell every loosened beam,
And, like a dam, the mighty wreck
　Lay right athwart the stream:
And a long shout of triumph
　Rose from the walls of Rome,
As to the highest turret-tops
　Was splashed the yellow foam.

And, like a horse unbroken
　When first he feels the rein,
The furious river struggled hard,
　And tossed his tawny mane,
And burst the curb, and bounded,
　Rejoicing to be free,
And whirling down, in fierce career,
Battlement, and plank, and pier,
　Rushed headlong to the sea.

Alone stood brave Horatius,
   But constant still in mind;
Thrice thirty thousand foes before,
   And the broad flood behind.
'Down with him!' cried false Sextus,
   With a smile on his pale face.
'Now yield thee,' cried Lars Porsena,
   'Now yield thee to our grace.'

Round turned he, as not deigning
   Those craven ranks to see;
Nought spake he to Lars Porsena,
   To Sextus nought spake he;
But he saw on Palatinus
   The white porch of his home;
And he spake to the noble river
   That rolls by the towers of Rome.

'Oh, Tiber! father Tiber!
   To whom the Romans pray,
A Roman's life, a Roman's arms,
   Take thou in charge this day!'
So he spake, and speaking sheathed
   The good sword by his side,
And with his harness on his back,
   Plunged headlong in the tide.

No sound of joy or sorrow
   Was heard from either bank;
But friends and foes in dumb surprise,
With parted lips and straining eyes,
   Stood gazing where he sank;
And when above the surges
   They saw his crest appear,
All Rome sent forth a rapturous cry,
And even the ranks of Tuscany
   Could scarce forbear to cheer.

But fiercely ran the current,
   Swollen high by months of rain:
And fast his blood was flowing;
   And he was sore in pain,
And heavy with his armour,
   And spent with changing blows:

And oft they thought him sinking,
  But still again he rose.

Never, I ween, did swimmer,
  In such an evil case,
Struggle through such a raging flood
  Safe to the landing place:
But his limbs were borne up bravely
  By the brave heart within,
And our good father Tiber
  Bare bravely up his chin.

'Curse on him!' quoth false Sextus;
  'Will not the villain drown?
But for this stay, ere close of day
  We should have sacked the town!'
'Heaven help him!' quoth Lars Porsena,
  'And bring him safe to shore;
For such a gallant feat of arms
  Was never seen before.'

And now he feels the bottom:
  Now on dry earth he stands;
Now round him throng the Fathers
  To press his gory hands;
And now, with shouts and clapping,
  And noise of weeping loud,
He enters through the River-Gate,
  Borne by the joyous crowd.

They gave him of the corn-land,
  That was of public right,
As much as two strong oxen
  Could plough from morn till night;
And they made a molten image,
  And set it up on high,
And there it stands unto this day
  To witness if I lie.

It stands in the Comitium,
  Plain for all folk to see;
Horatius in his harness,
  Halting upon one knee:

And underneath is written,
    In letters all of gold,
How valiantly he kept the bridge
    In the brave days of old.

And still his name sounds stirring
    Unto the men of Rome,
As the trumpet-blast that cries to them
    To charge the Volscian home;
And wives still pray to Juno
    For boys with hearts as bold
As his who kept the bridge so well
    In the brave days of old.

And in the nights of winter,
    When the cold north winds blow,
And the long howling of the wolves
    Is heard amidst the snow;
When round the lonely cottage
    Roars loud the tempest's din,
And the good logs of Algidus
    Roar louder yet within;

When the oldest cask is opened,
    And the largest lamp is lit;
When the chestnuts glow in the embers,
    And the kid turns on the spit;
When young and old in circle
    Around the firebrands close;
When the girls are weaving baskets,
    And the lads are shaping bows

When the goodman mends his armour,
    And trims his helmet's plume;
When the goodwife's shuttle merrily
    Goes flashing through the loom;
With weeping and with laughter
    Still is the story told,
How well Horatius kept the bridge
    In the brave days of old.

THOMAS BABINGTON MACAULAY

191

Signs of the Times

The Song of the Shirt

With fingers weary and worn,
  With eyelids heavy and red,
A woman sat, in unwomanly rags,
  Plying her needle and thread –
    Stitch – stitch – stitch!
In poverty, hunger, and dirt,
  And still with a voice of dolorous pitch
She sang the "Song of the Shirt!"

"Work – work – work!
While the cock is crowing aloof;
  And work – work – work
Till the stars shine through the roof!
It's oh! to be a slave
  Along with the barbarous Turk,
Where woman has never a soul to save,
  If this is Christian work!

"Work – work – work
Till the brain begins to swim;
  Work – work – work
Till the eyes are heavy and dim!
Seam, and gusset, and band, –
  Band, and gusset, and seam,
Till over the buttons I fall asleep,
  And sew them on in a dream!

"Oh! men with sisters dear!
  Oh! men with mothers and wives!
It is not linen you're wearing out,
  But human creatures' lives!
    Stitch – stitch – stitch,
In poverty, hunger, and dirt,
Sewing at once with a double thread
  A shroud as well as a shirt.

"But why do I talk of death!
    That phantom of grisly bone,
I hardly fear his terrible shape,
    It seems so like my own –
    It seems so like my own,
    Because of the fasts I keep;
O God! that bread should be so dear,
    And flesh and blood so cheap!

"Work – work – work!
    My labour never flags;
And what are its wages? A bed of straw,
    A crust of bread – and rags.
That shattered roof, – and this naked floor, –
    A table, – a broken chair, –
And a wall so blank, my shadow I thank
    For sometimes falling there.

"Work – work – work!
From weary chime to chime,
    Work – work – work
As prisoners work for crime!
    Band, and gusset, and seam,
    Seam, and gusset, and band,
Till the heart is sick, and the brain benumbed,
    As well as the weary hand.

"Work – work – work,
In the dull December light,
    And work – work – work,
When the weather is warm and bright; –
While underneath the eaves
    The brooding swallows cling,
As if to show me their sunny backs
    And twit me with the spring.

"Oh! but to breathe the breath
Of the cowslip and primrose sweet –
    With the sky above my head,
And the grass beneath my feet!
For only one short hour
    To feel as I used to feel,
Before I knew the woes of want
    And the walk that costs a meal!

193

"Oh! but for one short hour!
    A respite however brief!
No blessed leisure for love or hope,
    But only time for grief!
A little weeping would ease my heart,
    But in their briny bed
My tears must stop, for every drop
    Hinders needle and thread!"

With fingers weary and worn,
    With eyelids heavy and red,
A woman sat, in unwomanly rags,
    Plying her needle and thread –
        Stitch – stitch – stitch!
    In poverty, hunger, and dirt,
And still with a voice of dolorous pitch, –
Would that its tone could reach the rich! –
    She sang this "Song of the Shirt!"

THOMAS HOOD

The Leaden-Eyed

Let not young souls be smothered out before
They do quaint deeds and fully flaunt their pride.
It is the world's one crime its babes grow dull,
Its poor are ox-like, limp and leaden-eyed.

Not that they starve, but starve so dreamlessly,
Not that they sow, but that they seldom reap,
Not that they serve, but have no gods to serve,
Not that they die but that they die like sheep.

VACHEL LINDSAY

A Chartist Chorus

From *The Northern Star*, 6 June 1846

Go! cotton lords and corn lords, go!
　　Go! Ye live on loom and acre,
But let be seen – some law between
　　The giver and the taker.

Go! treasure well your miser's store
　　With crown, and cross, and sabre!
Despite you all – we'll break your thrall,
　　And have our land and labour.

You forge no more – you fold no more
　　Your cankering chains about us;
We heed you not – we need you not,
　　But you can't do without us.

You've lagged too long, the tide has turned,
　　Your helmsmen all were knavish;
And now we'll be – as bold and free,
　　As we've been tame and slavish.

Our lives are not your sheaves to glean –
　　Our rights your bales to barter:
Give all their own – from cot to throne,
　　But ours shall be THE CHARTER!

ERNEST JONES

The Devil's Thoughts

From his brimstone bed at break of day
A walking the Devil is gone,
To visit his snug little farm the earth,
And see how his stock goes on.

Over the hill and over the dale,
And he went over the plain,
And backward and forward he switched his long tail
As a gentleman switches his cane.

And how then was the Devil drest?
Oh! he was in his Sunday best:
His jacket was red and his breeches were blue,
And there was a hole where the tail came through.

He saw a Lawyer killing a Viper
On a dunghill hard by his own stable;
And the Devil smiled, for it put him in mind
Of Cain and his brother, Abel.

He saw an Apothecary on a white horse
    Ride by on his vocations,
And the Devil thought of his old Friend
    Death in the Revelations.

He saw a cottage with a double coach-house,
    A cottage of gentility;
And the Devil did grin, for his darling sin
    Is pride that apes humility.

He peep'd into a rich bookseller's shop,
    Quoth he! we are both of one college!
For I sate myself, like a cormorant, once
    Hard by the tree of knowledge.

Down the river did glide, with wind and tide,
    A pig with vast celerity;
And the Devil look'd wise as he saw how the while,
It cut its own throat. 'There!' quoth he with a smile,
    'Goes "England's commercial prosperity."'

As he went through Cold-Bath Fields he saw
    A solitary cell;
And the Devil was pleased, for it gave him a hint
    For improving his prisons in Hell.

He saw a Turnkey in a trice
    Fetter a troublesome blade;
'Nimbly,' quoth he, 'do the fingers move
    If a man be but used to his trade.'

He saw the same Turnkey unfetter a man,
    With but little expedition,
Which put him in mind of the long debate
    Of the Slave-trade abolition.

196

He saw an old acquaintance
   As he passed by a Methodist meeting; –
She holds a consecrated key,
   And the devil nods her a greeting.

She turned up her nose, and said,
   'Avaunt! my name's Religion,'
And she looked to Mr ———
   And leered like a love-sick pigeon.

He saw a certain minister
   (A minister to his mind)
Go up into a certain House,
   With a majority behind.

The Devil quoted Genesis
   Like a very learnéd clerk,
How 'Noah and his creeping things
   Went up into the Ark.'

He took from the poor,
   And he gave to the rich,
And he shook hands with a Scotchman,
   For he was not afraid of the ———

General ———————'s burning face
   He saw with consternation,
And back to hell his way did he take,
For the Devil thought by a slight mistake
   It was general conflagration.

           SAMUEL TAYLOR COLERIDGE

London

I wander thro' each charter'd street,
Near where the charter'd Thames does flow,
And mark in every face I meet
Marks of weakness, marks of woe.

In every cry of every Man,
In every Infant's cry of fear,
In every voice, in every ban,
The mind-forg'd manacles I hear.

How the Chimney-sweeper's cry
Every black'ning Church appalls;
And the hapless Soldier's sigh
Runs in blood down Palace walls.

But most thro' midnight streets I hear
How the youthful Harlot's curse
Blasts the new born Infant's tear,
And blights with plagues the Marriage hearse.

WILLIAM BLAKE

When Wilt Thou Save the People

When wilt Thou save the people?
  O God of mercy, when?
Not kings and lords, but nations!
  Not thrones and crowns, but men!
Flowers of Thy heart, O God, are they;
Let them not pass, like weeds, away,
Their heritage, a sunless day.
  God, save the people.

Shall crime bring crime forever,
  Strength aiding still the strong?
Is it Thy will, O Father,
  That man shall toil for wrong?
No, say Thy mountains; No, Thy skies;
Man's clouded sun shall brightly rise,
And songs ascend, instead of sighs.
  God, save the people!

When wilt Thou save the people?
  O God of mercy, when?
The people, Lord, the people,
  Not thrones and crowns, but men!

God, save the people, Thine they are,
Thy children as Thine angels fair.
From vice, oppression, and despair,
    God, save the people!

EBENEZER ELLIOTT

Sonnet 66

Tired with all these, for restful death I cry,
As, to behold desert a beggar born,
And needy nothing trimm'd in jollity,
And purest faith unhappily forsworn,
And gilded honour shamefully misplaced,
And maiden virtue rudely strumpeted,
And right perfection wrongfully disgraced,
And strength by limping sway disabled,
And art made tongue-tied by authority,
And folly, doctor-like, controlling skill,
And simple truth miscall'd simplicity,
And captive good attending captain ill:
    Tired with all these, from these would I be gone,
    Save that, to die, I leave my love alone.

WILLIAM SHAKESPEARE

'O Friend! I know not which way I must look'

O Friend! I know not which way I must look
For comfort, being, as I am, opprest,
To think that now our life is only drest
For show; mean handy-work of craftsman, cook,
Or groom! – We must run glittering like a brook
In the open sunshine, or we are unblest:
The wealthiest man among us is the best:
No grandeur now in nature or in book
Delights us. Rapine, avarice, expense,
This is idolatry; and these we adore:

Plain living and high thinking are no more:
The homely beauty of the good old cause
Is gone; our peace, our fearful innocence,
And pure religion breathing household laws.

WILLIAM WORDSWORTH

Report on Experience

I have been young, and now am not too old;
And I have seen the righteous forsaken,
His health, his honour and his quality taken.
    This is not what we were formerly told.

I have seen a green country, useful to the race,
Knocked silly with guns and mines, its villages vanished,
Even the last rat and the last kestrel banished –
    God bless us all, this was peculiar grace.

I knew Seraphina; Nature gave her hue,
Glance, sympathy, note, like one from Eden.
I saw her smile warp, heard her lyric deaden;
    She turned to harlotry; – this I took to be new.

Say what you will, our God sees how they run.
These disillusions are His curious proving
That He loves humanity and will go on loving;
    Over there are faith, life, virtue in the sun.

EDMUND BLUNDEN

September 1, 1939

I sit in one of the dives
On Fifty-Second Street
Uncertain and afraid
As the clever hopes expire
Of a low dishonest decade:
Waves of anger and fear
Circulate over the bright

200

And darkened lands of the earth,
Obsessing our private lives;
The unmentionable odour of death
Offends the September night.

Accurate scholarship can
Unearth the whole offence
From Luther until now
That has driven a culture mad,
Find what occurred at Linz,
What huge imago made
A psychopathic god:
I and the public know
What all schoolchildren learn,
Those to whom evil is done
Do evil in return.

Exiled Thucydides knew
All that a speech can say
About Democracy,
And what dictators do,
The elderly rubbish they talk
To an apathetic grave;
Analysed all in his book,
The enlightenment driven away,
The habit-forming pain,
Mismanagement and grief:
We must suffer them all again.

Into this neutral air
Where blind skyscrapers use
Their full height to proclaim
The strength of Collective Man,
Each language pours its vain
Competitive excuse:
But who can live for long
In an euphoric dream;
Out of the mirror they stare,
Imperialism's face
And the international wrong.

Faces along the bar
Cling to their average day:
The lights must never go out,

The music must always play,
All the conventions conspire
To make this fort assume
The furniture of home;
Lest we should see where we are,
Lost in a haunted wood,
Children afraid of the night
Who have never been happy or good.

The windiest militant trash
Important Persons shout
Is not so crude as our wish:
What mad Nijinsky wrote
About Diaghilev
Is true of the normal heart;
For the error bred in the bone
Of each woman and each man
Craves what it cannot have,
Not universal love
But to be loved alone.

From the conservative dark
Into the ethical life
The dense commuters come,
Repeating their morning vow,
'I *will* be true to the wife,
I'll concentrate more on my work',
And helpless governors wake
To resume their compulsory game:
Who can release them now,
Who can reach the deaf,
Who can speak for the dumb?

All I have is a voice
To undo the folded lie,
The romantic lie in the brain
Of the sensual man-in-the-street
And the lie of Authority
Whose buildings grope the sky:
There is no such thing as the State
And no one exists alone;
Hunger allows no choice
To the citizen or the police;
We must love one another or die.

Defenceless under the night
Our world in stupor lies;
Yet, dotted everywhere,
Ironic points of light
Flash out wherever the Just
Exchange their messages:
May I, composed like them
Of Eros and of dust,
Beleaguered by the same
Negation and despair,
Show an affirming flame.

W.H. AUDEN

Factory Windows Are always Broken

Factory windows are always broken.
Somebody's always throwing bricks,
Somebody's always heaving cinders,
Playing ugly Yahoo tricks.

Factory windows are always broken.
Other windows are let alone.
No one throws through the chapel-window
The bitter, snarling, derisive stone.

Factory windows are always broken.
Something or other is going wrong.
Something is rotten – I think, in Denmark.
End of the factory-window song.

VACHEL LINDSAY

Recessional

God of our fathers, known of old,
  Lord of our far-flung battle-line,
Beneath whose awful Hand we hold
  Dominion over palm and pine –
Lord God of Hosts, be with us yet,
Lest we forget – lest we forget!

The tumult and the shouting dies;
  The Captains and the Kings depart:
Still stands Thine ancient sacrifice,
  An humble and a contrite heart.
Lord God of Hosts, be with us yet,
Lest we forget – lest we forget!

Far-called, our navies melt away;
  On dune and headland sinks the fire:
Lo, all our pomp of yesterday
  Is one with Nineveh and Tyre!
Judge of the Nations, spare us yet,
Lest we forget – lest we forget!

If, drunk with sight of power, we loose
  Wild tongues that have not Thee in awe,
Such boastings as the Gentiles use,
  Or lesser breeds without the Law –
Lord God of Hosts, be with us yet,
Lest we forget – lest we forget!

For heathen heart that puts her trust
  In reeking tube and iron shard,
All valiant dust that builds on dust,
  And guarding, calls not Thee to guard,
For frantic boast and foolish word –
Thy mercy on Thy People, Lord!

RUDYARD KIPLING

Elegy in a Country Churchyard

The men that worked for England
They have their graves at home:
And bees and birds of England
About the cross can roam.

But they that fought for England,
Following a falling star,
Alas, alas for England
They have their graves afar.

And they that rule in England,
In stately conclave met,
Alas, alas for England
They have no graves as yet.

G.K. CHESTERTON

'The world is too much with us'

The world is too much with us; late and soon,
Getting and spending, we lay waste our powers:
Little we see in Nature that is ours;
We have given our hearts away, a sordid boon!
This Sea that bares her bosom to the moon;
The winds that will be howling at all hours,
And are up-gathered now like sleeping flowers;
For this, for everything, we are out of tune;
It moves us not. – Great God! I'd rather be
A Pagan suckled in a creed outworn;
So might I, standing on this pleasant lea,
Have glimpses that would make me less forlorn;
Have sight of Proteus rising from the sea;
Or hear old Triton blow his wreathèd horn.

WILLIAM WORDSWORTH

Ha'nacker Mill

Sally is gone that was so kindly
   Sally is gone from Ha'nacker Hill.
And the Briar grows ever since then so blindly
   And ever since then the clapper is still,
   And the sweeps have fallen from Ha'nacker Mill.

Ha'nacker Hill is in Desolation:
   Ruin a-top and a field unploughed.
And Spirits that call on a fallen nation
   Spirits that loved her calling aloud:
   Spirits abroad in a windy cloud.

Spirits that call and no one answers;
   Ha'nacker's down and England's done.
Wind and Thistle for pipe and dancers
   And never a ploughman under the Sun.
   Never a ploughman. Never a one.

HILAIRE BELLOC

'Farewell, rewards and fairies'

*A Proper New Ballad, entitled The Fairies' Farewell or God-a-Mercy
Will; to be sung or whistled to the tune of the Madow Brow by the
Learned; by the Unlearned, to the tune of Fortune.*

Farewell, rewards and fairies,
   Good housewives now may say,
For now foul sluts in dairies
   Do fare as well as they;
And though they sweep their hearths no less
   Than maids were wont to do,
Yet who of late for cleanliness
   Finds sixpence in her shoe?

Lament, lament old abbeys,
   The fairies lost command,
They did but change priests' babies,
   But some have chang'd your land;

And all your children stol'n from thence
   Are now grown puritanes
Who live as changelings ever since
   For love of your domains.

At morning and at evening both,
   You merry were and glad;
So little care of sleep and sloth
   These pretty ladies had;
When Tom came home from labour,
   Or Ciss to milking rose,
Then merrily went their tabor,
   And nimbly went their toes.

Witness those rings and roundelays
   Of theirs which yet remain,
Were footed in Queen Mary's days
   On many a grassy plain.
But since of late Elizabeth
   And later James came in,
They never danc'd on any heath
   As when the time had been.

By which we note the fairies
   Were of the old profession,
Their songs were *Ave Maries*,
   Their dances were procession;
But now alas, they all are dead
   Or gone beyond the seas,
Or further from religion fled,
   Or else they take their ease.

A tell-tale in their company
   They never could endure,
And whoso kept not secretly
   Their mirth, was punished sure.
It was a just and Christian deed
   To pinch such black and blue;
Oh, how the commonwealth doth need
   Such justices as you!

Now they have left our quarters,
   A register they have,
Who can preserve their charters,

A man both wise and grave.
A hundred of their merry pranks,
   By one that I could name
Are kept in store; con twenty thanks
   To William for the same.

To William Churne of Staffordshire
   Give laud and praises due;
Who every meal can mend your cheer
   With tales both old and true.
To William all give audience,
   And pray you for his noddle;
For all the fairies' evidence
   Were lost if it were addle.

RICHARD CORBET

The Sick Rose

O Rose, thou art sick!
The invisible worm
That flies in the night,
In the howling storm,

Has found out thy bed
Of crimson joy:
And his dark secret love
Does thy life destroy.

WILLIAM BLAKE

A New Jerusalem

'Would to God that all the Lord's people were Prophets.'
– Numbers, xi ch., 29 v.

And did those feet in ancient time
Walk upon England's mountains green?
And was the holy Lamb of God
On England's pleasant pastures seen?

And did the Countenance Divine
Shine forth upon our clouded hills?
And was Jerusalem builded here
Among these dark Satanic Mills?

Bring me my Bow of burning gold:
Bring me my Arrows of desire:
Bring me my Spear: O clouds unfold!
Bring me my Chariot of fire.

I will not cease from Mental Fight,
Nor shall my Sword sleep in my hand
Till we have built Jerusalem
In England's green & pleasant Land.

WILLIAM BLAKE

The Cry of the Children

Do ye hear the children weeping, O my brothers,
    Ere the sorrow comes with years?
They are leaning their young heads against their mothers,
    And *that* cannot stop their tears.
The young lambs are bleating in the meadows,
  The young birds are chirping in the nest,
The young fawns are playing with the shadows,
  The young flowers are blowing toward the west –
But the young, young children, O my brothers,
    They are weeping bitterly!
They are weeping in the playtime of the others,
    In the country of the free.

Do you question the young children in the sorrow
    Why their tears are falling so?
The old man may weep for his to-morrow
    Which is lost in Long Ago;
The old tree is leafless in the forest,
  The old year is ending in the frost,
The old wound, if stricken, is the sorest,
  The old hope is hardest to be lost:

But the young, young children, O my brothers,
      Do you ask them why they stand
Weeping sore before the bosoms of their mothers,
      In our happy Fatherland?

They look up with their pale and sunken faces,
      And their looks are sad to see,
For the man's hoary anguish draws and presses
      Down the cheeks of infancy;
"Your old earth," they say, "is very dreary,
  Our young feet," they say, "are very weak;
Few paces have we taken, yet are weary –
  Our grave-rest is very far to seek:
Ask the aged why they weep, and not the children,
      For the outside earth is cold,
And we young ones stand without, in our bewildering,
      And the graves are for the old.

"True," say the children, "it may happen
      That we die before our time:
Little Alice died last year, her grave is shapen
      Like a snowball, in the rime.
We looked into the pit prepared to take her:
  Was no room for any work in the close clay!
From the sleep wherein she lieth none will wake her,
  Crying, 'Get up, little Alice! it is day.'
If you listen by that grave, in sun and shower,
  With your ear down, little Alice never cries;
Could we see her face, be sure we should not know her,
  For the smile has time for growing in her eyes:
And merry go her moments, lulled and stilled in
      The shroud by the kirk-chime.
It is good when it happens," say the children,
      "That we die before our time."

Alas, alas, the children! they are seeking
      Death in life, as best to have:
They are binding up their hearts away from breaking,
      With a cerement from the grave.
Go out, children, from the mine and from the city,
  Sing out, children, as the little thrushes do;
Pluck your handfuls of the meadow-cowslips pretty,
  Laugh aloud, to feel your fingers let them through!

But they answer, "Are your cowslips of the meadows
     Like our weeds anear the mine?
Leave us quiet in the dark of the coal-shadows,
     From your pleasures fair and fine!

"For oh," say the children, "we are weary,
     And we cannot run or leap;
If we cared for any meadows, it were merely
     To drop down in them and sleep.
Our knees tremble sorely in the stooping,
   We fall upon our faces, trying to go;
And, underneath our heavy eyelids drooping
   The reddest flower would look as pale as snow.
For, all day, we drag our burden tiring
     Through the coal-dark, underground;
Or, all day, we drive the wheels of iron
     In the factories, round and round.

"For all day the wheels are droning, turning;
     Their wind comes in our faces,
Till our hearts turn, our heads with pulses burning,
     And the walls turn in their places:
Turns the sky in the high window, blank and reeling,
   Turns the long light that drops adown the wall,
Turn the black flies that crawl along the ceiling:
   All are turning, all the day, and we with all.
And all day the iron wheels are droning,
     And sometimes we could pray,
'O ye wheels' (breaking out in a mad moaning),
     'Stop! be silent for to-day!'"

Ay, be silent! Let them hear each other breathing
     For a moment, mouth to mouth!
Let them touch each other's hands, in a fresh wreathing
     Of their tender human youth!
Let them feel that this cold metallic motion
   Is not all the life God fashions or reveals:
Let them prove their living souls against the notion
   That they live in you, or under you, O wheels!
Still, all day, the iron wheels go onward,
     Grinding life down from its mark;
And the children's souls, which God is calling sunward,
     Spin on blindly in the dark.

Now tell the poor young children, O my brothers,
　　To look up to Him and pray;
So the blessed One who blesseth all the others,
　　Will bless them another day.
They answer, "Who is God that He should hear us,
　While the rushing of the iron wheels is stirred?
When we sob aloud, the human creatures near us
　Pass by, hearing not, or answer not a word.
And *we* hear not (for the wheels in their resounding)
　　Strangers speaking at the door:
Is it likely God, with angels singing round Him,
　　Hears our weeping any more?

"Two words, indeed, of praying we remember,
　　And at midnight's hour of harm,
'Our Father,' looking upwards in the chamber,
　　We say softly for a charm.
We know no other words except 'Our Father,'
　And we think that, in some pause of angels' song,
God may pluck them with the silence sweet to gather,
　And hold both within His right hand which is strong.
'Our Father!' If He heard us, He would surely
　　(For they call Him good and mild)
Answer, smiling down the steep world very purely,
　　'Come and rest with me, my child.'

"But, no!" say the children, weeping faster,
　　"He is speechless as a stone:
And they tell us, of His image is the master
　　Who commands us to work on.
Go to!" say the children, – "up in Heaven,
　Dark, wheel-like, turning clouds are all we find.
Do not mock us; grief has made us unbelieving:
　We look up for God, but tears have made us blind."
Do you hear the children weeping and disproving,
　　O my brothers, what ye preach?
For God's possible is taught by His world's loving,
　　And the children doubt of each.

And well may the children weep before you!
　　They are weary ere they run;
They have never seen the sunshine, nor the glory
　　Which is brighter than the sun.

They know the grief of man, without its wisdom;
  They sink in man's despair, without its calm;
Are slaves, without the liberty in Christdom,
  Are martyrs, by the pang without the palm:
Are worn as if with age, yet unretrievingly
    The harvest of its memories cannot reap, –
Are orphans of the earthly love and heavenly.
    Let them weep! let them weep!

They look up with their pale and sunken face,
    And their look is dread to see,
For they mind you of their angels in high places,
    With eyes turned on Deity.
"How long," they say, "how long, O cruel nation,
  Will you stand, to move the world, on a child's heart, –
Stifle down with a mailed heel its palpitation,
  And tread onward to your throne amid the mart?
Our blood splashes upward, O gold-heaper,
    And your purple shows your path!
But the child's sob in the silence curses deeper
    Than the strong man in his wrath."

ELIZABETH BARRETT BROWNING

The Secret People

Call upon the wheels, master, call upon the wheels,
Weary grow the holidays when you miss the meals,
Through the Gate of Treason, through the gate within,
Cometh fear and greed of fame, cometh deadly sin;
If a man grow faint, master, take him ere he kneels,
Take him, break him, rend him, end him, roll him,
    crush him with the wheels.

Smile at us, pay us, pass us; but do not quite forget;
For we are the people of England, that never have spoken yet.
There is many a fat farmer that drinks less cheerfully,
There is many a free French peasant who is richer and sadder
    than we.
There are no folk in the whole world so helpless or so wise.
There is hunger in our bellies, there is laughter in our eyes;

213

You laugh at us and love us, both mugs and eyes are wet:
Only you do not know us. For we have not spoken yet.

The fine French kings came over in a flutter of flags and dames.
We liked their smiles and battles, but we never could say their
  names.
The blood ran red to Bosworth and the high French lords went
  down;
There was naught but a naked people under a naked crown.
And the eyes of the King's Servants turned terribly every way,
And the gold of the King's Servants rose higher every day.
They burnt the homes of the shaven men, that had been quaint
  and kind,
Till there was no bed in a monk's house, nor food that man could
  find.
The inns of God where no man paid, that were the wall of the
  weak,
The King's Servants ate them all. And still we did not speak.

And the face of the King's Servants grew greater than the King:
He tricked them, and they trapped him, and stood round him in
  a ring.
The new grave lords closed round him, that had eaten the abbey's
  fruits,
And the men of the new religion, with their bibles in their boots,
We saw their shoulders moving, to menace or discuss,
And some were pure and some were vile; but none took heed
  of us.
We saw the King as they killed him, and his face was proud and
  pale;
And a few men talked of freedom, while England talked of ale.

A war that we understood not came over the world and woke
Americans, Frenchmen, Irish; but we knew not the things they
  spoke.
They talked about rights and nature and peace and the people's
  reign:
And the squires, our masters, bade us fight; and scorned us never
  again.
Weak if we be for ever, could none condemn us then;
Men called us serfs and drudges; men knew that we were men.
In foam and flame at Trafalgar, on Albuera plains,
We did and died like lions, to keep ourselves in chains
We lay in living ruins; firing and fearing not

214

The strange fierce face of the Frenchmen who knew for what they
    fought,
And the man who seemed to be more than man we strained
    against and broke;
And we broke our own rights with him. And still we never spoke.

Our patch of glory ended; we never heard guns again.
But the squire seemed struck in the saddle; he was foolish, as if
    in pain.
He leaned on a staggering lawyer, he clutched a cringing Jew,
He was stricken; it may be, after all, he was stricken at Waterloo.
Or perhaps the shades of the shaven men, whose spoil is in his
    house,
Come back in shining shapes at last to spoil his last carouse:
We only know the last sad squires ride slowly towards the sea,
And a new people takes the land: and still it is not we.

They have given us into the hand of new unhappy lords,
Lords without anger and honour, who dare not carry their
    swords.
They fight by shuffling papers; they have bright dead alien eyes;
They look at our labour and laughter as a tired man looks at flies.
And the load of their loveless pity is worse than the ancient
    wrongs,
Their doors are shut in the evening; and they know no songs.

We hear men speaking for us of new laws strong and sweet,
Yet is there no man speaketh as we speak in the street.
It may be we shall rise the last as Frenchmen rose the first,
Our wrath come after Russia's wrath and our wrath be the worst.
It may be we are meant to mark with our riot and our rest
God's scorn for all men governing. It may be beer is best.
But we are the people of England; and we have not spoken yet.
Smile at us, pay us, pass us. But do not quite forget.

G.K. CHESTERTON

The Song of the Lower Classes

We plough and sow – we're so very, very low
   That we delve in the dirty clay,
Till we bless the plain with the golden grain,
   And the vale with the fragrant hay.
Our place we know – we're so very low,
   'Tis down at the landlord's feet:
We're not too low the bread to grow,
   But too low the bread to eat.

Down, down we go – we're so very, very low,
   To the hell of the deep-sunk mines,
But we gather the proudest gems that glow
   When the crown of a despot shines.
And, whenever he lacks, upon our backs
   Fresh loads he deigns to lay:
We're far too low to vote the tax,
   But not too low to pay.

We're low – we're low – mere rabble, we know,
   But at our plastic power,
The mould at the lordling's feet will grow
   Into palace and church and tower.
Then prostrate fall in the rich man's hall,
   And cringe at the rich man's door:
We're not too low to build the wall,
   But too low to tread the floor.

We're low – we're low – we're very, very low,
   Yet from our fingers glide
The silken flow – and the robes that glow
   Round the limbs of the sons of pride.
And what we get – and what we give –
   We know, and we know our share:
We're not too low the cloth to weave,
   But too low the cloth to wear!

We're low – we're low – we're very, very low,
   And yet when the trumpets ring,
The thrust of a poor man's arm will go
   Thro' the heart of the proudest king.

We're low – we're low – our place we know,
  We're only the rank and file,
We're not too low to kill the foe,
  But too low to touch the spoil.

ERNEST JONES

Gentlemen-Rankers

To the legion of the lost ones, to the cohort of the damned,
  To my brethren in their sorrow overseas,
Sings a gentleman of England cleanly bred, machinely crammed,
  And a trooper of the Empress, if you please.
Yes, a trooper of the forces who has run his own six horses,
  And faith he went the pace and went it blind,
And the world was more than kin while he held the ready tin,
  But to-day the Sergeant's something less than kind.
      We're poor little lambs who've lost our way,
        Baa! Baa! Baa!
      We're little black sheep who've gone astray,
        Baa – aa – aa!
      Gentlemen-rankers out on the spree,
      Damned from here to Eternity,
      God ha' mercy on such as we,
        Baa! Yah! Bah!

Oh, it's sweet to sweat through stables, sweet to empty kitchen
    slops,
  And it's sweet to hear the tales the troopers tell,
To dance with blowzy housemaids at the regimental hops
  And thrash the cad who says you waltz too well.
Yes, it makes you cock-a-hoop to be 'Rider' to your troop,
  And branded with a blasted worsted spur,
When you envy, O how keenly, one poor Tommy living cleanly
  Who blacks your boots and sometimes calls you 'Sir.'

If the home we never write to, and the oaths we never keep,
  And all we know most distant and most dear,
Across the snoring barrack-room return to break our sleep,
  Can you blame us if we soak ourselves in beer?

217

When the drunken comrade mutters and the great guard-lantern
     gutters
   And the horror of our fall is written plain,
Every secret, self-revealing on the aching whitewashed ceiling,
   Do you wonder that we drug ourselves from pain?

We have done with Hope and Honour, we are lost to Love and
     Truth,
   We are dropping down the ladder rung by rung,
And the measure of our torment is the measure of our youth.
   God help us, for we knew the worst too young!
Our shame is clean repentance for the crime that brought the
     sentence,
   Our pride it is to know no spur of pride,
And the Curse of Reuben holds us till an alien turf enfolds us
   And we die, and none can tell Them where we died.
          We're poor little lambs who've lost our way,
              Baa! Baa! Baa!
          We're little black sheep who've gone astray,
              Baa – aa – aa!
          Gentlemen-rankers out on the spree,
          Damned from here to Eternity,
          God ha' mercy on such as we,
              Baa! Yah! Bah!

RUDYARD KIPLING

The Second Coming

     Turning and turning in the widening gyre
     The falcon cannot hear the falconer;
     Things fall apart; the centre cannot hold;
     Mere anarchy is loosed upon the world,
     The blood-dimmed tide is loosed, and everywhere
     The ceremony of innocence is drowned;
     The best lack all conviction, while the worst
     Are full of passionate intensity.

     Surely some revelation is at hand;
     Surely the Second Coming is at hand.
     The Second Coming! Hardly are those words out
     When a vast image out of *Spiritus Mundi*

Troubles my sight: somewhere in sands of the desert
A shape with lion body and the head of a man,
A gaze blank and pitiless as the sun,
Is moving its slow thighs, while all about it
Reel shadows of the indignant desert birds.
The darkness drops again; but now I know
That twenty centuries of stony sleep
Were vexed to nightmare by a rocking cradle,
And what rough beast, its hour come round at last,
Slouches towards Bethlehem to be born?

W.B. YEATS

Gone for a Soldier

In Flanders Fields

In Flanders fields the poppies blow
Between the crosses, row on row
    That mark our place; and in the sky
    The larks, still bravely singing, fly
Scarce heard amid the guns below.

We are the Dead. Short days ago
We lived, felt dawn, saw sunset glow,
    Loved and were loved, and now we lie
        In Flanders fields.

Take up our quarrel with the foe:
To you from failing hands we throw
    The torch; be yours to hold it high.
    If ye break faith with us who die
We shall not sleep, though poppies grow
        In Flanders fields.

JOHN McCRAE

Does It Matter?

Does it matter? – losing your legs?...
For people will always be kind,
And you need not show that you mind
When the others come in after hunting
To gobble their muffins and eggs.

Does it matter? – losing your sight?...
There's such splendid work for the blind;
And people will always be kind,
As you sit on the terrace remembering
And turning your face to the light.

Do they matter? – those dreams from the pit?...
You can drink and forget and be glad,
And people won't say that you're mad;
For they'll know that you've fought for your country,
And no one will worry a bit.

SIEGFRIED SASSOON

Battle Hymn of the American Republic

Mine eyes have seen the glory of the coming of the Lord:
He is trampling out the vintage where the grapes of wrath are
    stored;
He hath loosed the fatal lightning of his terrible swift sword:
        His truth is marching on.

I have seen him in the watch-fires of a hundred circling camps;
They have builded him an altar in the evening dews and damps;
I can read his righteous sentence by the dim and flaring lamps:
        His day is marching on.

I have read a fiery gospel, writ in burnish'd rows of steel:
'As ye deal with my contemners, so with you my grace shall deal;
Let the Hero, born of woman, crush the serpent with his heel!
        Since God is marching on.'

He has sounded forth the trumpet that shall never call retreat;
He is sifting out the hearts of men before his Judgment Seat;
O, be swift, my soul to answer Him, be jubilant my feet!
        Our God is marching on.

In the beauty of the lilies Christ was born, across the sea,
With a glory in his bosom that transfigures you and me:
As He died to make men holy, let us die to make men free,
        While God is marching on.

JULIA WARD HOWE

A Lament for Flodden

I've heard them lilting at our ewe-milking,
  Lasses a' lilting before dawn o' day;
But now they are moaning on ilka green loaning –
  The Flowers of the Forest are a' wede away.

At bughts, in the morning, nae blythe lads are scorning,
  Lasses are lonely and dowie and wae;
Nae daffing, nae gabbing, but sighing and sabbing,
  Ilk ane lifts her leglin and hies her away.

In hairst, at the shearing, nae youths now are jeering,
  Bandsters are lyart, and runkled, and gray:
At fair or at preaching, nae wooing, nae fleeching –
  The Flowers of the Forest are a' wede away.

At e'en, in the gloaming, nae swankies are roaming
  'Bout stacks wi' the lasses at bogle to play;
But ilk ane sits eerie, lamenting her dearie –
  The Flowers of the Forest are a' wede away.

Dool and wae for the order sent our lads to the Border!
  The English, for ance, by guile wan the day;
The Flowers of the Forest, that fought aye the foremost,
  The prime of our land, lie cauld in the clay.

We'll hear nae mair lilting at our ewe-milking;
  Women and bairns are heartless and wae;
Sighing and moaning on ilka green loaning –
  The Flowers of the Forest are a' wede away.

JEAN ELLIOT

For the Fallen

With proud thanksgiving, a mother for her children,
England mourns for her dead across the sea.
Flesh of her flesh they were, spirit of her spirit,
Fallen in the cause of the free.

Solemn the drums thrill: Death august and royal
Sings sorrow up into immortal spheres.
There is music in the midst of desolation
And a glory that shines upon our tears.

They went with songs to the battle, they were young,
Straight of limb, true of eye, steady and aglow.
They were staunch to the end against odds uncounted,
They fell with their faces to the foe.

They shall grow not old, as we that are left grow old:
Age shall not weary them, nor the years condemn.
At the going down of the sun and in the morning
We will remember them.

They mingle not with their laughing comrades again;
They sit no more at familiar tables of home;
They have no lot in our labour of the day-time;
They sleep beyond England's foam.

But where our desires are and our hopes profound,
Felt as a well-spring that is hidden from sight,
To the innermost heart of their own land they are known
As the stars are known to the Night;

As the stars that shall be bright when we are dust,
Moving in marches upon the heavenly plain,
As the stars that are starry in the time of our darkness,
To the end, to the end, they remain.

LAURENCE BINYON

Danny Deever

'What are the bugles blowin' for?' said Files-on-Parade.
'To turn you out, to turn you out,' the Colour-Sergeant said.
'What makes you look so white, so white?' said Files-on-Parade.
'I'm dreadin' what I've got to watch,' the Colour-Sergeant said.
    For they're hangin' Danny Deever, you can hear the Dead
        March play,
    The Regiment's in 'ollow square – they're hangin' him to-day;

They've taken of his buttons off an' cut his stripes away,
An' they're hangin' Danny Deever in the mornin'.

'What makes the rear-rank breathe so 'ard?' said Files-on-Parade.
'It's bitter cold, it's bitter cold,' the Colour-Sergeant said.
'What makes that front-rank man fall down?' said Files-on-Parade.
'A touch o' sun, a touch o' sun,' the Colour-Sergeant said.
    They are hangin' Danny Deever, they are marchin' of 'im
        round.
    They 'ave 'alted Danny Deever by 'is coffin on the ground;
    An' 'e'll swing in 'arf a minute for a sneakin' shootin' hound –
    O they're hangin' Danny Deever in the mornin'!'

''Is cot was right-'and cot to mine,' said Files-on-Parade.
''E's sleepin' out an' far to-night,' the Colour-Sergeant said.
'I've drunk 'is beer a score o' times,' said Files-on-Parade.
''E's drinkin' bitter beer alone,' the Colour-Sergeant said.
    They are hangin' Danny Deever, you must mark 'im to 'is
        place,
    For 'e shot a comrade sleepin' – you must look 'im in the face;
    Nine 'undred of 'is county an' the Regiment's disgrace,
    While they're hangin' Danny Deever in the mornin'.

'What's that so black agin the sun?' said Files-on-Parade.
'It's Danny fightin' 'ard for life,' the Colour-Sergeant said.
'What's that that whimpers over 'ead?' said Files-on-Parade.
'It's Danny's soul that's passin' now,' the Colour-Sergeant said.
    For they're done with Danny Deever, you can 'ear the quick-
        step play,
    The Regiment's in column, an' they're marchin' us away;
    Ho! the young recruits are shakin', an' they'll want their beer
        to-day,
    After hangin' Danny Deever in the mornin'!

RUDYARD KIPLING

Mine Sweepers
1914-18

Dawn off the Foreland – the young flood making
   Jumbled and short and steep –
Black in the hollows and bright where it's breaking –
   Awkward water to sweep.
   'Mines reported in the fairway,
   'Warn all traffic and detain.
'Sent up *Unity, Claribel, Assyrian, Stormcock,* and *Golden Gain.*'

Noon off the Foreland – the first ebb making
   Lumpy and strong in the bight.
Boom after boom, and the golf-hut shaking
   And the jackdaws wild with fright!
   'Mines located in the fairway,
   'Boats now working up the chain,
'Sweepers – *Unity, Claribel, Assyrian, Stormcock,* and *Golden Gain.*'

Dusk off the Foreland – the last light going
   And the traffic crowding through,
And five damned trawlers with their syreens blowing
   Heading the whole review!
   'Sweep completed in the fairway.
   'No more mines remain.
'Sent back *Unity, Claribel, Assyrian, Stormcock,* and *Golden Gain.*'

RUDYARD KIPLING

We Be Soldiers Three

We be soldiers three,
   Pardona moy, je vous an pree,
Lately come forth of the Low Country,
   With never a penny of money.

Here, good fellow, I drink to thee,
   Pardona moy, je vous an pree,
To all good fellows, wherever they be,
   With never a penny of money.

And he that will not pledge me thus,
 Pardona moy, je vous an pree,
Pays for the shot, whatever it is,
 With never a penny of money.

Charge it again, boy, charge it again,
 Pardona moy, je vous an pree,
As long as there is any ink in thy pen,
 With never a penny of money.

ANON

Naming of Parts

Today we have naming of parts. Yesterday,
We had daily cleaning. And tomorrow morning,
We shall have what to do after firing. But today,
Today we have naming of parts. Japonica
Glistens like coral in all of the neighbour gardens,
 And today we have naming of parts.

This is the lower sling swivel. And this
Is the upper sling swivel, whose use you will see,
When you are given your slings. And this is the piling swivel,
Which in your case you have not got. The branches
Hold in the gardens their silent, eloquent gestures,
 Which in our case we have not got.

This is the safety-catch, which is always released
With an easy flick of the thumb. And please do not let me
See anyone using his finger. You can do it quite easy
If you have any strength in your thumb. The blossoms
Are fragile and motionless, never letting anyone see
 Any of them using their finger.

And this you can see is the bolt. The purpose of this
Is to open the breech, as you see. We can slide it
Rapidly backwards and forwards: we call this
Easing the spring. And rapidly backwards and forwards
The early bees are assaulting and fumbling the flowers:
 They call it easing the Spring.

They call it easing the Spring: it is perfectly easy
If you have any strength in your thumb: like the bolt,
And the breech, and the cocking-piece, and the point of balance,
Which in our case we have not got; and the almond blossom
Silent in all of the gardens and the bees going backwards and
       forwards,
    For today we have naming of parts.

HENRY REED

For Johnny

Do not despair
For Johnny-head-in-air;
He sleeps as sound
As Johnny underground.

Fetch out no shroud
For Johnny-in-the-cloud;
And keep your tears
For him in after years.

Better by far
For Johnny-the-bright-star,
To keep your head,
And see his children fed.

JOHN PUDNEY

Parting in Wartime

How long ago Hector took off his plume,
Not wanting that his little son should cry,
Then kissed his sad Andromache goodbye –
And now we three in Euston waiting-room.

FRANCES CORNFORD

Epitaph on an Army of Mercenaries

These, in the day when heaven was falling,
  The hour when earth's foundations fled,
Followed their mercenary calling
  And took their wages and are dead.

Their shoulders held the sky suspended;
  They stood, and earth's foundations stay;
What God abandoned, these defended,
  And saved the sum of things for pay.

A.E. HOUSMAN

Here Dead Lie We

Here dead lie we because we did not choose
  To live and shame the land from which we sprung.
Life, to be sure, is nothing much to lose;
  But young men think it is, and we were young.

A.E. HOUSMAN

The Battle of Blenheim

It was a summer evening,
  Old Kaspar's work was done,
And he before his cottage door
  Was sitting in the sun,
And by him sported on the green
His little grandchild Wilhelmine.

She saw her brother Peterkin
  Roll something large and round,
Which he beside the rivulet
  In playing there had found;
He came to ask what he had found,
That was so large, and smooth, and round.

228

Old Kaspar took it from the boy,
    Who stood expectant by;
And then the old man shook his head,
    And with a natural sigh,
"'T is some poor fellow's skull," said he,
"Who fell in the great victory.

"I find them in the garden,
    For there's many here about;
And often when I go to plough,
    The ploughshare turns them out!
For many thousand men," said he,
"Were slain in that great victory."

"Now tell us what 't was all about,"
    Young Peterkin, he cries;
And little Wilhelmine looks up
    With wonder-waiting eyes;
"Now tell us all about the war,
And what they fought each other for."

"It was the English," Kaspar cried,
    "Who put the French to rout;
But what they fought each other for,
    I could not well make out;
But every body said," quoth he,
"That 't was a famous victory.

"My father lived at Blenheim then,
    Yon little stream hard by;
They burnt his dwelling to the ground,
    And he was forced to fly;
So with his wife and child he fled,
Nor had he where to rest his head.

"With fire and sword the country round
    Was wasted far and wide,
And many a childing mother then,
    And new-born baby died;
But things like that, you know, must be
At every famous victory.

"They say it was a shocking sight
   After the field was won;
For many thousand bodies here
   Lay rotting in the sun;
But things like that, you know, must be
After a famous victory.

"Great praise the Duke of Marlbro' won,
   And our good Prince Eugene."
"Why 't was a very wicked thing!"
   Said little Wilhelmine.
"Nay..nay..my little girl," quoth he,
"It was a famous victory.

"And every body praised the Duke
   Who this great fight did win."
"But what good came of it at last?"
   Quoth little Peterkin.
"Why that I cannot tell," said he,
"But 't was a famous victory."

ROBERT SOUTHEY

The Destruction of Sennacherib

The Assyrian came down like the wolf on the fold,
And his cohorts were gleaming in purple and gold;
And the sheen of their spears was like stars on the sea,
When the blue wave rolls nightly on deep Galilee.

Like the leaves of the forest when Summer is green,
That host with their banners at sunset were seen:
Like the leaves of the forest when Autumn hath blown,
That host on the morrow lay withered and strown.

For the angel of Death spread his wings on the blast,
And breathed in the face of the foe as he passed;
And the eyes of the sleepers waxed deadly and chill,
And their hearts but once heaved – and for ever grew still!

And there lay the steed with his nostril all wide,
But through it there rolled not the breath of his pride;
And the foam of his gasping lay white on the turf,
And cold as the spray of the rock-beating surf.

And there lay the rider distorted and pale,
With the dew on his brow, and the rust on his mail:
And the tents were all silent – the banners alone –
The lances unlifted – the trumpet unblown.

And the widows of Ashur are loud in their wail,
And the idols are broke in the temple of Baal;
And the might of the Gentile, unsmote by the sword,
Hath melted like snow in the glance of the Lord!

GEORGE GORDON, LORD BYRON

War Song of the Saracens

We are they who come faster than fate: we are they who ride early
    or late:
We storm at your ivory gate: Pale Kings of the Sunset, beware!
Not on silk nor in samet we lie, not in curtained solemnity die
Among women who chatter and cry, and children who mumble
    a prayer.
But we sleep by the ropes of the camp, and we rise with a shout,
    and we tramp
With the sun or the moon for a lamp, and the spray of the wind
    in our hair.

From the lands, where the elephants are, to the forts of Merou
    and Balghar,
Our steel we have brought and our star to shine on the ruins of
    Rum.
We have marched from the Indus to Spain, and by God we will
    go there again;
We have stood on the shore of the plain where the Waters of
    Destiny boom.
A mart of destruction we made at Jalula where men were afraid,
For death was a difficult trade, and the sword was a broker of
    doom;

And the Spear was a Desert Physician who cured not a few of
    ambition,
And drave not a few to perdition with medicine bitter and strong:
And the shield was a grief to the fool and as bright as a desolate
    pool,
And as straight as the rock of Stamboul when their cavalry
    thundered along:
For the coward was drowned with the brave when our battle
    sheered up like a wave,
And the dead to the desert we gave, and the glory to God in our
    song.

JAMES ELROY FLECKER

The General

'Good-morning; good-morning!' the General said
When we met him last week on our way to the line.
Now the soldiers he smiled at are most of 'em dead,
And we're cursing his staff for incompetent swine.
'He's a cheery old card,' grunted Harry to Jack
As they slogged up to Arras with rifle and pack.
   .   .   .   .   .

But he did for them both by his plan of attack.

SIEGFRIED SASSOON

Accidie

The Dykes

We have no heart for the fishing – we have no hand for the oar –
All that our fathers taught us of old pleases us now no more.
All that our own hearts bid us believe we doubt where we do not
     deny –
There is no proof in the bread we eat nor rest in the toil we ply.

Look you, our foreshore stretches far through sea-gate, dyke, and
     groin –
Made land all, that our fathers made, where the flats and the
     fairway join.
They forced the sea a sea-league back. They died, and their work
     stood fast.
We were born to peace in the lee of the dykes, but the time of our
     peace is past.

Far off, the full tide clambers and slips, mouthing and testing all,
Nipping the flanks of the water-gates, baying along the wall;
Turning the shingle, returning the shingle, changing the set of
     the sand...
We are too far from the beach, men say, to know how the outworks
     stand.

So we come down, uneasy, to look; uneasily pacing the beach.
These are the dykes our fathers made: we have never known a
     breach.
Time and again has the gale blown by and we were not afraid;
Now we come only to look at the dykes – at the dykes our fathers
     made.

O'er the marsh where the homesteads cower apart the harried
     sunlight flies,
Shifts and considers, wanes and recovers, scatters and sickens
     and dies –
An evil ember bedded in ash – a spark blown west by the wind...
We are surrendered to night and the sea – the gale and the tide
     behind!

233

At the bridge of the lower saltings the cattle gather and blare,
Roused by the feet of running men, dazed by the lantern-glare.
Unbar and let them away for their lives – the levels drown as they
stand,
Where the flood-wash forces the sluices aback and the ditches
deliver inland.

Ninefold deep to the top of the dykes the galloping breakers
stride,
And their overcarried spray is a sea – a sea on the landward side.
Coming, like stallions they paw with their hooves, going they
snatch with their teeth,
Till the bents and the furze and the sand are dragged out, and the
old-time hurdles beneath.

Bid men gather fuel for fire, the tar, the oil, and the tow –
Flame we shall need, not smoke, in the dark if the riddled sea-
banks go.
Bid the ringers watch in the tower (who knows how the dawn
shall prove?)
Each with his rope between his feet and the trembling bells above.

Now we can only wait till the day, wait and apportion our shame.
These are the dykes our fathers left, but we would not look to
the same.
Time and again were we warned of the dykes, time and again we
delayed:
Now, it may fall, we have slain our sons, as our fathers we have
betrayed.

Walking along the wreck of the dykes, watching the work of the
seas!
These were the dykes our fathers made to our great profit and
ease.
But the peace is gone and the profit is gone, with the old sure
days withdrawn...
That our own houses show as strange when we come back in the
dawn!

RUDYARD KIPLING

The Pessimist

Nothing to do but work,
  Nothing to eat but food,
Nothing to wear but clothes,
  To keep one from going nude.

Nothing to breathe but air,
  Quick as a flash 'tis gone;
Nowhere to fall but off,
  Nowhere to stand but on.

Nothing to comb but hair,
  Nowhere to sleep but in bed,
Nothing to weep but tears,
  Nothing to bury but dead.

Nothing to sing but songs,
  Ah, well, alas! alack!
Nowhere to go but out,
  Nowhere to come but back.

Nothing to see but sights,
  Nothing to quench but thirst,
Nothing to have but what we've got.
  Thus through life we are cursed.

Nothing to strike but a gait;
  Everything moves that goes.
Nothing at all but common sense
  Can ever withstand these woes.

BEN KING

I Am

I am: yet what I am none cares or knows,
  My friends forsake me like a memory lost;
I am the self-consumer of my woes,
  They rise and vanish in oblivious host,
Like shades in love and death's oblivion lost;
And yet I am, and live with shadows tost

235

Into the nothingness of scorn and noise,
   Into the living sea of waking dreams,
Where there is neither sense of life nor joys,
   But the vast shipwreck of my life's esteems;
And e'en the dearest – that I loved the best –
Are strange – nay, rather stranger than the rest.

I long for scenes where man has never trod,
   A place where woman never smiled or wept;
There to abide with my Creator, God,
   And sleep as I in childhood sweetly slept:
Untroubling and untroubled where I lie
The grass below – above the vaulted sky.

JOHN CLARE

Sorrow of Mydath

Weary the cry of the wind is, weary the sea,
Weary the heart and the mind and the body of me.
Would I were out of it, done with it, would I could be
   A white gull crying along the desolate sands!

Outcast, derelict soul in a body accurst,
Standing drenched with the spindrift, standing athirst,
For the cool green waves of death to arise and burst
   In a tide of quiet for me on the desolate sands.

Would that the waves and the long white hair of the spray
Would gather in splendid terror and blot me away
To the sunless place of the wrecks where the waters sway
   Gently, dreamily, quietly over desolate sands!

JOHN MASEFIELD

Mirage

The hope I dreamed of was a dream,
  Was but a dream; and now I wake,
Exceeding comfortless, and worn, and old,
  For a dream's sake.

I hang my harp upon a tree,
  A weeping willow in a lake;
I hang my silenced harp there, wrung and snapt
  For a dream's sake.

Lie still, lie still, my breaking heart;
  My silent heart, lie still and break:
Life, and the world, and mine own self are changed
  For a dream's sake.

CHRISTINA ROSSETTI

A Pause of Thought

I looked for that which is not, nor can be,
  And hope deferred made my heart sick in truth:
  But years must pass before a hope of youth
    Is resigned utterly.

I watched and waited with a steadfast will:
  And though the object seemed to flee away
  That I so longed for, ever day by day
    I watched and waited still.

Sometimes I said: 'This thing shall be no more;
  My expectation wearies and shall cease;
  I will resign it now and be at peace':
    Yet never gave it o'er.

Sometimes I said: 'It is an empty name
  I long for; to a name why should I give
  The peace of all the days I have to live?' –
    Yet gave it all the same.

Alas thou foolish one! alike unfit
  For healthy joy and salutary pain:
  Thou knowest the chase useless, and again
    Turnest to follow it.

CHRISTINA ROSSETTI

The Departure of the good Dæmon

What can I do in Poetry,
Now the good Spirit's gone from me?
Why nothing now, but lonely sit,
And over-read what I have writ.

ROBERT HERRICK

Spleen

I was not sorrowful, I could not weep,
And all my memories were put to sleep.

I watched the river grow more white and strange,
All day till evening I watched it change.

All day till evening I watched the rain
Beat wearily upon the window pane.

I was not sorrowful, but only tired
Of everything that ever I desired.

Her lips, her eyes, all day became to me
The shadow of a shadow utterly.

All day mine hunger for her heart became
Oblivion, until the evening came,

238

And left me sorrowful, inclined to weep,
With all my memories that could not sleep.

ERNEST DOWSON

'All, all of a piece throughout'

All, all of a piece throughout:
Thy Chase had a Beast in view:
Thy Wars brought nothing about;
Thy Lovers were all untrue.
'Tis well an Old Age is out,
And time to begin a New.

JOHN DRYDEN

Time Passing

Birthright

Lord Rameses of Egypt sighed
  Because a summer evening passed;
And little Ariadne cried
  That summer fancy fell at last
To dust; and young Verona died
  When beauty's hour was overcast.

Theirs was the bitterness we know
  Because the clouds of hawthorn keep
So short a state, and kisses go
  To tombs unfathomably deep,
While Rameses and Romeo
  And little Ariadne sleep.

JOHN DRINKWATER

'All the flowers of the spring'

All the flowers of the spring
Meet to perfume our burying:
These have but their growing prime,
And man does flourish but his time.
Survey our progress from our birth,
We are set, we grow, we turn to earth.

Courts adieu, and all delights,
All bewitching appetites;
Sweetest breath, and clearest eye,
Like perfumes go out and die;
And consequently this is done,
As shadows wait upon the sun.
Vain the ambition of kings,
Who seek by trophies and dead things,

To leave a living name behind,
And weave but nets to catch the wind.
O you have wrought a miracle, and melted
A heart of adamant: you have compris'd
In this dumb pageant, a right excellent form
Of penitence.

JOHN WEBSTER

'Egypt's might is tumbled down'

Egypt's might is tumbled down
   Down a-down the deeps of thought;
Greece is fallen and Troy town,
Glorious Rome hath lost her crown,
   Venice' pride is nought.

But the dreams their children dreamed
   Fleeting, unsubstantial, vain.
Shadowy as the shadows seemed
Airy nothing, as they deemed,
   These remain.

MARY COLERIDGE

On Wenlock Edge

On Wenlock Edge the wood's in trouble;
   His forest fleece the Wrekin heaves;
The gale, it plies the saplings double,
   And thick on Severn snow the leaves.

'Twould blow like this through holt and hanger
   When Uricon the city stood:
'Tis the old wind in the old anger,
   But then it threshed another wood.

Then, 'twas before my time, the Roman
    At yonder heaving hill would stare:
The blood that warms an English yeoman,
    The thoughts that hurt him, they were there.

There, like the wind through woods in riot,
    Through him the gale of life blew high;
The tree of man was never quiet:
    Then 'twas the Roman, now 'tis I.

The gale, it plies the saplings double,
    It blows so hard, 'twill soon be gone:
Today the Roman and his trouble
    Are ashes under Uricon.

A.E. HOUSMAN

Cities and Thrones and Powers

Cities and Thrones and Powers,
        Stand in Time's eye,
Almost as long as flowers,
        Which daily die.
But, as new buds put forth
        To glad new men,
Out of the spent and unconsidered Earth
        The Cities rise again.

This season's Daffodil,
        She never hears
What change, what chance, what chill,
        Cut down last year's:
But with bold countenance,
        And knowledge small,
Esteems her seven days' continuance
        To be perpetual.

So Time that is o'er-kind,
  To all that be,
Ordains us e'en as blind,
  As bold as she:
That in our very death,
  And burial sure,
Shadow to shadow, well persuaded, saith,
  "See how our works endure!"

RUDYARD KIPLING

Cargoes

Quinquireme of Nineveh from distant Ophir,
Rowing home to haven in sunny Palestine,
With a cargo of ivory,
And apes and peacocks,
Sandalwood, cedarwood, and sweet white wine.

Stately Spanish galleon coming from the Isthmus,
Dipping through the Tropics by the palm-green shores,
With a cargo of diamonds,
Emeralds, amethysts,
Topazes, and cinnamon, and gold moidores.

Dirty British coaster with a salt-caked smoke stack,
Butting through the Channel in the mad March days,
With a cargo of Tyne coal,
Road-rails, pig-lead,
Firewood, iron-ware, and cheap tin trays.

JOHN MASEFIELD

'Go and catch a falling star'

Go and catch a falling star,
  Get with child a mandrake root,
Tell me where all past years are,
  Or who cleft the Devil's foot;
Teach me to hear mermaids singing,
Or to keep off envy's stinging,
    And find
    What wind
Serves to advance an honest mind.

If thou be'st born to strange sights,
  Things invisible to see,
Ride ten thousand days and nights
  Till Age snow white hairs on thee;
Thou, when thou return'st, wilt tell me
All strange wonders that befell thee,
    And swear
    No where
Lives a woman true and fair.

If thou find'st one, let me know;
  Such a pilgrimage were sweet.
Yet do not; I would not go,
  Though at next door we might meet.
Though she were true when you met her,
And last till you write your letter,
    Yet she
    Will be
False, ere I come, to two or three.

JOHN DONNE

Sic Vita

  Like to the falling of a star;
  Or as the flights of eagles are;
  Or like the fresh spring's gaudy hue;
  Or silver drops of morning dew;

Or like a wind that chafes the flood;
Or bubbles which on water stood;
Even such is man, whose borrowed light
Is straight called in, and payed to night.

The wind blows out, the bubble dies;
The spring entombed in Autumn lies:
The dew dries up: the star is shot:
The flight is past: and man forgot.

HENRY KING

Ozymandias

I met a traveller from an antique land
Who said: Two vast and trunkless legs of stone
Stand in the desert... Near them, on the sand,
Half sunk, a shattered visage lies, whose frown,
And wrinkled lip, and sneer of cold command,
Tell that its sculptor well those passions read
Which yet survive, stamped on these lifeless things,
The hand that mocked them, and the heart that fed:
And on the pedestal these words appear:
'My name is Ozymandias, king of kings:
Look on my works, ye Mighty, and despair!'
Nothing beside remains. Round the decay
Of that colossal wreck, boundless and bare
The lone and level sands stretch far away.

PERCY BYSSHE SHELLEY

'Time, you old gipsy man'

Time, you old gipsy man,
Will you not stay,
Put up your caravan
Just for one day?

All things I'll give you
Will you be my guest,
Bells for your jennet
Of silver the best,
Goldsmiths shall beat you
A great golden ring
Peacocks shall bow to you,
Little boys sing,
Oh, and sweet girls will
Festoon you with may.
Time, you old gipsy,
Why hasten away?

Last week in Babylon,
Last night in Rome,
Morning, and in the crush
Under Paul's dome;
Under Paul's dial
You tighten your rein –
Only a moment,
And off once again;
Off to some city
Now blind in the womb,
Off to another
Ere that's in the tomb.

Time, you old gipsy man,
Will you not stay,
Put up your caravan
Just for one day?

RALPH HODGSON

In Time of 'the Breaking of Nations'

Only a man harrowing clods
    In a slow silent walk
With an old horse that stumbles and nods
    Half asleep as they stalk.

246

Only thin smoke without flame
    From the heaps of couch-grass;
Yet this will go onward the same
    Though Dynasties pass.

Yonder a maid and her wight
    Come whispering by:
War's annals will cloud into night
    Ere their story die.

THOMAS HARDY

The Old Ships

I have seen old ships sail like swans asleep
Beyond the village which men still call Tyre,
With leaden age o'ercargoed, dipping deep
For Famagusta and the hidden sun
That rings black Cyprus with a lake of fire;
And all those ships were certainly so old
Who knows how oft with squat and noisy gun,
Questing brown slaves or Syrian oranges,
The pirate Genoese
Hell-raked them till they rolled
Blood, water, fruit and corpses up the hold.
But now through friendly seas they softly run,
Painted the mid-sea blue or shore-sea green,
Still patterned with the vine and grapes in gold.

But I have seen,
Pointing her shapely shadows from the dawn
And image tumbled on a rose-swept bay,
A drowsy ship of some yet older day;
And, wonder's breath indrawn,
Thought I – who knows – who knows – but in that same
(Fished up beyond Ææa, patched up new
– Stern painted brighter blue –)
That talkative, bald-headed seaman came
(Twelve patient comrades sweating at the oar)
From Troy's doom-crimson shore,
And with great lies about his wooden horse
Set the crew laughing, and forgot his course.

247

It was so old a ship – who knows, who knows?
– And yet so beautiful, I watched in vain
To see the mast burst open with a rose,
And the whole deck put on its leaves again.

JAMES ELROY FLECKER

'How soon hath time...'

How soon hath time the subtle thief of youth,
    Stol'n on his wing my three and twentieth year!
My hasting days fly on with full career,
    But my late spring no bud or blossom sheweth.
Perhaps my semblance might deceive the truth,
    That I to manhood am arrived so near,
    And inward ripeness doth much less appear,
    That some more timely-happy spirits endueth.
Yet be it less or more, or soon or slow,
    It shall be still in strictest measure even,
    To that same lot, however mean or high,
Toward which time leads me, and the will of heaven;
    All is, if I have grace to use it so,
    As ever in my great task-master's eye.

JOHN MILTON

Coronemus nos Rosis antequam marcescant

Let us drink and be merry, dance, joke, and rejoice,
With claret and sherry, theorbo and voice!
The changeable world to our joy is unjust,
        All treasure 's uncertain,
        Then down with your dust!
In frolics dispose your pounds, shillings, and pence,
For we shall be nothing a hundred years hence.

We'll sport and be free with Moll, Betty, and Dolly,
Have oysters and lobsters to cure melancholy:
Fish-dinners will make a lass spring like a flea,
    Dame Venus, love's lady,
    Was born of the sea;
With her and with Bacchus we'll tickle the sense,
For we shall be past it a hundred years hence.

Your most beautiful bride who with garlands is crown'd
And kills with each glance as she treads on the ground,
Whose lightness and brightness doth shine in such splendour
    That none but the stars
    Are thought fit to attend her,
Though now she be pleasant and sweet to the sense,
Will be damnable mouldy a hundred years hence.

Then why should we turmoil in cares and in fears,
Turn all our tranquill'ty to sighs and to tears?
Let's eat, drink, and play till the worms do corrupt us,
    'Tis certain, *Post mortem*
    Nulla voluptas.
For health, wealth and beauty, wit, learning and sense,
Must all come to nothing a hundred years hence.

THOMAS JORDAN

'You are old, Father William'

'You are old, Father William,' the young man said,
  'And your hair has become very white;
And yet you incessantly stand on your head –
  Do you think, at your age, it is right?'

'In my youth,' Father William replied to his son,
  'I feared it might injure the brain;
But, now that I'm perfectly sure I have none,
  Why, I do it again and again.'

'You are old,' said the youth, 'as I mentioned before,
  And have grown most uncommonly fat;
Yet you turned a back-somersault in at the door –
  Pray, what is the reason of that?'

249

'In my youth,' said the sage, as he shook his grey locks,
   'I kept all my limbs very supple
By the use of this ointment – one shilling the box –
   Allow me to sell you a couple?'

'You are old,' said the youth, 'and your jaws are too weak
   For anything tougher than suet;
Yet you finished the goose, with the bones and the beak –
   Pray, how did you manage to do it?'

'In my youth,' said his father, 'I took to the law,
   And argued each case with my wife;
And the muscular strength, which it gave to my jaw,
   Has lasted the rest of my life.'

'You are old,' said the youth, 'one would hardly suppose
   That your eye was as steady as ever;
Yet you balance an eel on the end of your nose –
   What made you so awfully clever?'

'I have answered three questions, and that is enough,'
   Said his father. 'Don't give yourself airs!
Do you think I can listen all day to such stuff?
   Be off, or I'll kick you down-stairs!'

LEWIS CARROLL

Ode

We are the music-makers,
   And we are the dreamers of dreams,
Wandering by lone sea-breakers,
   And sitting by desolate streams;
World-losers and world-forsakers,
   On whom the pale moon gleams:
Yet we are the movers and shakers
   Of the world for ever, it seems.

With wonderful deathless ditties
We build up the world's great cities,
  And out of a fabulous story
  We fashion an empire's glory:
One man with a dream, at pleasure,
  Shall go forth and conquer a crown;
And three with a new song's measure
  Can trample an empire down.

We, in the ages lying
  In the buried past of the earth,
Built Nineveh with our sighing,
  And Babel itself with our mirth;
And o'erthrew them with prophesying
  To the old of the new world's worth;
For each age is a dream that is dying,
  Or one that is coming to birth.

                    ARTHUR O'SHAUGHNESSY

Piazza Piece

– I am a gentleman in a dustcoat trying
To make you hear. Your ears are soft and small
And listen to an old man not at all,
They want the young men's whispering and sighing.
But see the roses on your trellis dying
And hear the spectral singing of the moon;
For I must have my lovely lady soon,
I am a gentleman in a dustcoat trying.

– I am a lady young in beauty waiting
Until my truelove comes, and then we kiss.
But what grey man among the vines is this
Whose words are dry and faint as in a dream?
Back from my trellis, Sir, before I scream!
I am a lady young in beauty waiting.

                    JOHN CROWE RANSOM

251

First Fig

My candle burns at both ends;
  It will not last the night;
But ah, my foes, and oh, my friends –
  It gives a lovely light!

EDNA ST VINCENT MILLAY

Deaths and Endings

On My First Son

Farewell, thou child of my right hand, and joy;
  My sin was too much hope of thee, loved boy.
Seven years thou wert lent to me, and I thee pay,
  Exacted by thy fate, on the just day.
Oh, could I lose all father now! For why
  Will man lament the state he should envy?
To have so soon 'scaped world's and flesh's rage,
  And, if no other misery, yet age?
Rest in soft peace, and, asked, say here doth lie
  Ben Jonson his best piece of poetry;
For whose sake, henceforth, all his vows be such,
  As what he loves may never like too much.

BEN JONSON

Death the Leveller

The glories of our blood and state
  Are shadows, not substantial things;
There is no armour against Fate;
  Death lays his icy hand on kings:
    Sceptre and Crown
    Must tumble down,
And in the dust be equal made
With the poor crooked scythe and spade.

Some men with swords may reap the field,
  And plant fresh laurels where they kill:
But their strong nerves at last must yield;
  They tame but one another still:
    Early or late
    They stoop to fate,
And must give up their murmuring breath
When they, pale captives, creep to death.

253

The garlands wither on your brow;
   Then boast no more your mighty deeds!
Upon Death's purple altar now
   See where the victor-victim bleeds.
         Your heads must come
         To the cold tomb:
Only the actions of the just
Smell sweet and blossom in their dust.

JAMES SHIRLEY

Dying Speech of an Old Philosopher

I strove with none, for none was worth my strife;
   Nature I loved, and, next to Nature, Art;
I warmed both hands before the fire of Life;
   It sinks, and I am ready to depart.

WALTER SAVAGE LANDOR

'There's been a Death...'

There's been a Death, in the Opposite House,
As lately as Today –
I know it, by the numb look
Such Houses have – alway –

The Neighbors rustle in and out –
The Doctor – drives away –
A Window opens like a Pod –
Abrupt – mechanically –

Somebody flings a Mattress out –
The Children hurry by –
They wonder if it died – on that –
I used to – when a Boy –

The Minister – goes stiffly in –
As if the House were His –
And He owned all the Mourners – now –
And little Boys – besides –

And then the Milliner – and the Man
Of the Appalling Trade –
To take the measure of the House –

There'll be that Dark Parade –

Of Tassels – and of Coaches – soon –
It's easy as a Sign –
The Intuition of the News –
In just a Country Town –

EMILY DICKINSON

Friends Beyond

William Dewy, Tranter Reuben, Farmer Ledlow late at plough,
    Robert's kin, and John's, and Ned's,
And the Squire, and Lady Susan, lie in Mellstock churchyard now!

'Gone,' I call them, gone for good, that group of local hearts and
    heads;
    Yet at mothy curfew-tide,
And at midnight when the noon-heat breathes it back from walls
    and leads,

They've a way of whispering to me – fellow-wight who yet abide –
    In the muted, measured note
Of a ripple under archways, or a lone cave's stillicide:

'We have triumphed: this achievement turns the bane to antidote,
    Unsuccesses to success,
Many thought-worn eves and morrows to a morrow free of thought.

'No more need we corn and clothing, feel of old terrestrial stress;
    Chill detraction stirs no sigh;
Fear of death has even bygone us: death gave all that we possess.'

W.D. – 'Ye mid burn the old bass-viol that I set such value by.'
Squire. – 'You may hold the manse in fee,
    You may wed my spouse, may let my children's memory of
        me die.'

Lady S. – 'You may have my rich brocades, my laces; take each
        household key;
    Ransack coffer, desk, bureau;
    Quiz the few poor treasures hid there, con the letters kept
        by me.'

Far. – 'Ye mid zell my favourite heifer, ye mid let the charlock
        grow,
    Foul the grinterns, give up thrift.'
Far. Wife. – 'If ye break my best blue china, children, I shan't care
    or ho.'

All. – 'We've no wish to hear the tidings, how the people's fortunes
        shift;
    What your daily doings are;
    Who are wedded, born, divided; if your lives beat slow or
        swift.

    'Curious not the least are we if our intents you make or mar,
        If you quire to our old tune,
    If the City stage still passes, if the weirs still roar afar.'

    – Thus, with very gods' composure, freed those crosses late
        and soon
        Which, in life, the Trine allow
    (Why, none witteth), and ignoring all that haps beneath the
        moon,

    William Dewy, Tranter Reuben, Farmer Ledlow late at plough,
        Robert's kin, and John's, and Ned's,
    And the Squire, and Lady Susan, murmur mildly to me now.

                              THOMAS HARDY

Dirge Without Music

I am not resigned to the shutting away of loving hearts in the hard
    ground.
So it is, and so it will be, for so it has been, time out of mind:
Into the darkness they go, the wise and the lovely. Crowned
With lilies and with laurel they go; but I am not resigned.

Lovers and thinkers, into the earth with you.
Be one with the dull, the indiscriminate dust.
A fragment of what you felt, of what you knew,
A formula, a phrase remains, – but the best is lost.

The answers quick and keen, the honest look, the laughter, the
    love, –
They are gone. They are gone to feed the roses. Elegant and curled
Is the blossom. Fragrant is the blossom. I know. But I do not
    approve.
More precious was the light in your eyes than all the roses in the
    world.

Down, down, down into the darkness of the grave
Gently they go, the beautiful, the tender, the kind;
Quietly they go, the intelligent, the witty, the brave.
I know. But I do not approve. And I am not resigned.

EDNA ST VINCENT MILLAY

The Bridge of Sighs

One more unfortunate,
Weary of breath,
Rashly importunate,
Gone to her death!

Take her up tenderly,
Lift her with care;
Fashioned so slenderly,
Young, and so fair!

Look at her garments
Clinging like cerements
Whilst the wave constantly
Drips from her clothing;
Take her up instantly,
Loving, not loathing.

Touch her not scornfully;
Think of her mournfully,
Gently and humanly;
Not of the stains of her;
All that remains of her
Now is pure womanly.

Make no deep scrutiny
Into her mutiny
Rash and undutiful;
Past all dishonour,
Death has left on her
Only the beautiful.

Still, for all slips of hers,
One of Eve's family –
Wipe those poor lips of hers,
Oozing so clammily.

Loop up her tresses,
Escaped from the comb,
Her fair auburn tresses;
Whilst wonderment guesses
Where was her home?

Who was her father?
Who was her mother?
Had she a sister?
Had she a brother?
Or was there a dearer one
Still, and a nearer one
Yet, than all other?

Alas! for the rarity
Of Christian charity
Under the sun!
Oh! it was pitiful!

Near a whole city full,
Home she had none!

Sisterly, brotherly,
Fatherly, motherly,
Feelings had changed:
Love, by harsh evidence,
Thrown from its eminence;
Even God's providence
Seeming estranged.

Where the lamps quiver
So far in the river,
With many a light
From window and casement,
From garret to basement,
She stood, with amazement,
Houseless by night.

The bleak wind of March
Made her tremble and shiver;
But not the dark arch,
Or the black flowing river.
Mad from life's history,
Glad to death's mystery,
Swift to be hurled –
Anywhere, anywhere,
Out of the world!

In she plunged boldly,
No matter how coldly
The rough river ran, –
Over the brink of it,
Picture it – think of it,
Dissolute man!
Lave in it, drink of it,
Then, if you can!

Take her up tenderly,
Lift her with care;
Fashioned so slenderly,
Young, and so fair!

Ere her limbs frigidly
Stiffen too rigidly,
Decently, kindly,
Smooth and compose them.
And her eyes, close them,
Staring so blindly!

Dreadfully staring
Through muddy impurity,
As when with the daring
Last look of despairing,
Fixed on futurity.

Perishing gloomily,
Spurred by contumely,
Cold inhumanity,
Burning insanity,
Into her rest.
Cross her hands humbly,
As if praying dumbly,
Over her breast!

Owning her weakness,
Her evil behaviour,
And leaving, with meekness,
Her sins to her Saviour!

THOMAS HOOD

'Adieu! farewell earth's bliss!'

Adieu! farewell earth's bliss!
This world uncertain is:
Fond are life's lustful joys,
Death proves them all but toys.
None from his darts can fly:
I am sick, I must die.
    Lord, have mercy on us!

Rich men, trust not in wealth!
Gold cannot buy your health;
Physic himself must fade;
All things to end are made;
The plague full swift goes by:
I am sick, I must die.
    Lord, have mercy on us!

Beauty is but a flower
Which wrinkles will devour:
Brightness falls from the air;
Queens have died young and fair;
Dust hath closed Helen's eye:
I am sick, I must die.
    Lord, have mercy on us!

Strength stoops unto the grave,
Worms feed on Hector brave,
Swords may not fight with fate,
Earth still holds ope her gate.
Come, come, the bells do cry,
I am sick, I must die.
    Lord, have mercy on us!

Wit with his wantonness
Tasteth death's bitterness:
Hell's executioner
Hath no ears for to hear
What vain art can reply:
I am sick, I must die.
    Lord, have mercy on us!

Haste, therefore, each degree
To welcome destiny:
Heaven is our heritage,
Earth but a player's stage:
Mount we unto the sky.
I am sick. I must die.
    Lord, have mercy on us!

THOMAS NASHE

Crossing the Bar

Sunset and evening star,
  And one clear call for me!
And may there be no moaning of the bar,
  When I put out to sea,

But such a tide as moving seems asleep,
  Too full for sound and foam,
When that which drew from out the boundless deep
  Turns again home.

Twilight and evening bell,
  And after that the dark!
And may there be no sadness of farewell,
  When I embark;

For though from out our bourne of Time and Place
  The flood may bear me far,
I hope to see my Pilot face to face
  When I have crost the bar.

ALFRED, LORD TENNYSON

Afterwards

When the Present has latched its postern behind my tremulous
    stay,
  And the May month flaps its glad green leaves like wings,
Delicate-filmed as new-spun silk, will the neighbours say,
  'He was a man who used to notice such things'?

If it be in the dusk when, like an eyelid's soundless blink,
  The dewfall-hawk comes crossing the shades to alight
Upon the wind-warped upland thorn, a gazer may think,
  'To him this must have been a familiar sight.'

If I pass during some nocturnal blackness, mothy and warm,
  When the hedgehog travels furtively over the lawn,
One may say, 'He strove that such innocent creatures should
    come to no harm,
  But he could do little for them; and now he is gone.'

If, when hearing that I have been stilled at last, they stand at the
    door,
  Watching the full-starred heavens that winter sees,
Will this thought rise on those who will meet my face no more,
  'He was one who had an eye for such mysteries'?

And will any say when my bell of quittance is heard in the gloom,
  And a crossing breeze cuts a pause in its outrollings,
Till they swell again, as they were a new bell's boom,
  'He hears it not now, but used to notice such things'?

THOMAS HARDY

'Tell me not here...'

Tell me not here, it needs not saying,
  What tune the enchantress plays
In aftermaths of soft September
  Or under blanching mays,
For she and I were long acquainted
  And I knew all her ways.

On russet floors, by waters idle,
  The pine lets fall its cone;
The cuckoo shouts all day at nothing
  In leafy dells alone;
And traveller's joy beguiles in autumn
  Hearts that have lost their own.

On acres of the seeded grasses
  The changing burnish heaves;
Or marshalled under moons of harvest
  Stand still all night the sheaves;
Or beeches strip in storms for winter
  And stain the wind with leaves.

Possess, as I possessed a season,
  The countries I resign,
Where over elmy plains the highway
  Would mount the hills and shine,
And full of shade the pillared forest
  Would murmur and be mine.

For nature, heartless, witless nature,
  Will neither care nor know
What stranger's feet may find the meadow
  And trespass there and go,
Nor ask amid the dews of morning
  If they are mine or no.

A.E. HOUSMAN

'Fear no more the heat o'th'sun'

Fear no more the heat o'th'sun,
  Nor the furious winter's rages;
Thou thy worldly task hast done,
  Home art gone and ta'en thy wages.
Golden lads and girls all must,
As chimney-sweepers, come to dust.

Fear no more the frown o'th'great;
  Thou art past the tyrant's stroke;
Care no more to clothe and eat;
  To thee the reed is as the oak.
The sceptre, learning, physic, must
All follow this and come to dust.

Fear no more the lightning flash,
  Nor th'all-dreaded thunder-stone;
Fear not slander, censure rash;
  Thou hast finished joy and moan.
All lovers young, all lovers must
Consign to thee and come to dust.

No exorciser harm thee!
Nor no witchcraft charm thee!
Ghost unlaid forbear thee!
Nothing ill come near thee!
Quiet consummation have;
And renownéd be thy grave!

WILLIAM SHAKESPEARE

Not Waving but Drowning

Nobody heard him, the dead man,
But still he lay moaning:
I was much further out than you thought
And not waving but drowning.

Poor chap, he always loved larking
And now he's dead
It must have been too cold for him his heart gave way,
They said.

Oh, no no no, it was too cold always
(Still the dead one lay moaning)
I was much too far out all my life
And not waving but drowning.

STEVIE SMITH

The Old Familiar Faces

I have had playmates, I have had companions,
In my days of childhood, in my joyful school-days,
All, all are gone, the old familiar faces.

I have been laughing, I have been carousing,
Drinking late, sitting late, with my bosom cronies,
All, all are gone, the old familiar faces.

I loved a love once, fairest among women;
Closed are her doors on me, I must not see her –
All, all are gone, the old familiar faces.

I have a friend, a kinder friend has no man;
Like an ingrate, I left my friend abruptly;
Left him, to muse on the old familiar faces.

Ghost-like I paced round the haunts of my childhood.
Earth seem'd a desert I was bound to traverse,
Seeking to find the old familiar faces.

Friend of my bosom, thou more than a brother,
Why wert not thou born in my father's dwelling?
So might we talk of the old familiar faces –

How some they have died, and some they have left me,
And some are taken from me; all are departed;
All, all are gone, the old familiar faces.

CHARLES LAMB

On a Sleeping Friend

Lady, when your lovely head
Droops to sink among the Dead,
And the quiet places keep
You that so divinely sleep;
Then the dead shall blessèd be
With a new solemnity,
For such a Beauty, so descending,
Pledges them that Death is ending.
Sleep your fill – but when you wake
Dawn shall over Lethe break.

HILAIRE BELLOC

'When lately Pym descended into hell'

When lately Pym descended into hell,
Ere he the cups of Lethe did carouse,
What place that was, he called loud to tell;
To whom a devil, "This is the lower house."

WILLIAM DRUMMOND OF HAWTHORNDEN

The Dog from Malta

translated from the Greek of Tymnès

He came from Malta, and Eumelus says
He had no dog like him in all his days;
We called him Bull; he went into the dark;
Along those roads we cannot hear him bark.

EDMUND BLUNDEN

The Exequy

Accept thou shrine of my dead saint,
Instead of dirges this complaint;
And for sweet flowers to crown thy hearse,
Receive a strew of weeping verse
From thy grieved friend, whom thou mightst see
Quite melted into tears for thee.

Dear loss! since thy untimely fate
My task hath been to meditate
On thee, on thee: thou art the book,
The library whereon I look
Though almost blind. For thee (loved clay)
I languish out, not live the day,
Using no other exercise
But what I practise with mine eyes:
By which wet glasses I find out
How lazily time creeps about
To one that mourns: this, only this
My exercise and business is:
So I compute the weary hours
With sighs dissolvèd into showers.

Nor wonder if my time go thus
Backward and most preposterous;
Thou hast benighted me, thy set
This eve of blackness did beget,
Who wast my day, (though overcast
Before thou hadst thy Noon-tide past)
And I remember must in tears,

267

Thou scarce hadst seen so many years
As day tells hours. By thy clear sun
My love and fortune first did run;
But thou wilt never more appear
Folded within my hemisphere,
Since both thy light and motion
Like a fled star is fallen and gone,
And 'twixt me and my soul's dear wish
The earth now interposèd is,
Which such a strange eclipse doth make
As ne'er was read in almanack.

I could allow thee for a time
To darken me and my sad clime,
Were it a month, a year, or ten,
I would thy exile live till then;
And all that space my mirth adjourn,
So thou wouldst promise to return;
And putting off thy ashy shroud
At length disperse this sorrow's cloud.

But woe is me! the longest date
Too narrow is to calculate
These empty hopes: never shall I
Be so much blest as to descry
A glimpse of thee, till that day come
Which shall the earth to cinders doom,
And a fierce fever must calcine
The body of this world like thine,
(My little world!); that fit of fire
Once off, our bodies shall aspire
To our souls' bliss: then shall we rise,
And view our selves with clearer eyes
In that calm region, where no night
Can hide us from each other's sight.

Meantime, thou hast her, earth: much good
May my harm do thee. Since it stood
With Heaven's will I might not call
Her longer mine, I give thee all
My short-lived right and interest
In her, whom living I loved best:
With a most free and bounteous grief,
I give thee what I could not keep.

Be kind to her, and prithee look
Thou write into thy Doomsday book
Each parcel of this rarity
Which in thy casket shrined doth ly:
See that thou make thy reckoning straight,
And yield her back again by weight;
For thou must audit on thy trust
Each graine and atome of this dust,
As thou wilt answer him that lent,
Not gave thee, my dear monument.

So close the ground, and 'bout her shade
Black curtains draw, my Bride is laid.

Sleep on my Love in thy cold bed
Never to be disquieted!
My last good night! Thou wilt not wake
Till I thy fate shall overtake:
Till age, or grief, or sickness must
Marry my body to that dust
It so much loves; and fill the room
My heart keeps empty in thy tomb.
Stay for me there; I will not fail
To meet thee in that hollow vale.
And think not much of my delay;
I am already on the way,
And follow thee with all the speed
Desire can make, or sorrows breed.
Each minute is a short degree,
And every hour a step towards thee.
At night when I betake to rest,
Next morn I rise nearer my west
Of life, almost by eight hours sail,
Than when sleep breathed his drowsy gale.

Thus from the sun my bottom steers,
And my day's compass downward bears:
Nor labour I to stem the tide
Through which to Thee I swiftly glide.

'Tis true, with shame and grief I yield,
Thou like the Van first took'st the field,
And gotten hast the victory
In thus adventuring to die

Before me, whose more years might crave
A just precedence in the grave.
But hark! My pulse like a soft drum
Beats my approach, tells Thee I come;
And slow howe'er my marches be,
I shall at last sit down by Thee.

   The thought of this bids me go on,
And wait my dissolution
With hope and comfort. Dear (forgive
The crime) I am content to live
Divided, with but half a heart,
Till we shall meet and never part.

HENRY KING

'Even such is Time...'

Even such is Time, which takes in trust
Our youth, our joys, and all we have,
And pays us but with age and dust;
Who in the dark and silent grave,
When we have wandered all our ways,
Shuts up the story of our days.
But from which earth and grave and dust
The Lord shall raise me up, I trust.

SIR WALTER RALEGH

Upon the Death of Sir Albert Morton's Wife

He first deceased; she for a little tried
To live without him, liked it not, and died.

SIR HENRY WOTTON

On the Tombs in Westminster Abbey

Mortality, behold and fear
What a change of flesh is here!
Think how many royal bones
Sleep within these heaps of stones;
Here they lie, had realms and lands,
Who now want strength to stir their hands,
Where from their pulpits seal'd with dust
They preach, 'In greatness is no trust.'
Here's an acre sown indeed
With the richest royallest seed
That the earth did e'er suck in
Since the first man died for sin:
Here the bones of birth have cried
'Though gods they were, as men they died!'
Here are sands, ignoble things,
Dropt from the ruin'd sides of kings:
Here's a world of pomp and state
Buried in dust, once dead by fate.

SIR FRANCIS BEAUMONT

The Death Bed

We watch'd her breathing thro' the night,
  Her breathing soft and low,
As in her breast the wave of life
  Kept heaving to and fro.

So silently we seem'd to speak,
  So slowly moved about,
As we had lent her half our powers
  To eke her living out.

Our very hopes belied our fears,
  Our fears our hopes belied –
We thought her dying when she slept,
  And sleeping when she died.

271

For when the morn came dim and sad
And chill with early showers,
Her quiet eyelids closed – she had
Another morn than ours.

THOMAS HOOD

Cold in the Earth

Cold in the earth, and the deep snow piled above thee!
Far, far removed, cold in the dreary grave!
Have I forgot, my Only Love, to love thee,
Severed at last by Time's all-wearing wave?

Now, when alone, do my thoughts no longer hover
Over the mountains on Angora's shore;
Resting their wings where heath and fern-leaves cover
That noble heart for ever, ever more?

Cold in the earth, and fifteen wild Decembers
From those brown hills have melted into spring –
Faithful indeed is the spirit that remembers
After such years of change and suffering!

Sweet Love of youth, forgive if I forget thee
While the World's tide is bearing me along:
Sterner desires and darker hopes beset me,
Hopes which obscure but cannot do thee wrong.

No other Sun has lightened up my heaven;
No other Star has ever shone for me:
All my life's bliss from thy dear life was given –
All my life's bliss is in the grave with thee.

But when the days of golden dreams had perished
And even Despair was powerless to destroy,
Then did I learn how existence could be cherished,
Strengthened and fed without the aid of joy;

Then did I check the tears of useless passion,
Weaned my young soul from yearning after thine;
Sternly denied its burning wish to hasten
Down to that tomb already more than mine!

And even yet, I dare not let it languish,
Dare not indulge in Memory's rapturous pain;
Once drinking deep of that divinest anguish,
How could I seek the empty world again?

EMILY BRONTË

Requiem

Under the wide and starry sky
Dig the grave and let me lie:
Glad did I live and gladly die,
   And I laid me down with a will.

This be the verse you grave for me:
Here he lies where he long'd to be;
Home is the sailor, home from sea,
   And the hunter home from the hill.

ROBERT LOUIS STEVENSON

On Prince Frederick

Here lies Fred
Who was alive and is dead.
Had it been his father,
I had much rather;
Had it been his brother,
Still better than another;
Had it been his sister,
No one would have missed her;

Had it been the whole generation,
So much the better for the nation;
But since 'tis only Fred
Who was alive and is dead,
Why, there's no more to be said.

ANON

Extempore Epitaph
(Uttered at Charles's insistence)

Here lies a great and mighty king
  Whose promise none relies on;
He never said a foolish thing,
  Nor ever did a wise one.

JOHN WILMOT, EARL OF ROCHESTER

'Hark, now every thing is still'

Hark, now every thing is still,
The screech-owl and the whistler shrill
Call upon our Dame, aloud,
And bid her quickly don her shroud.
Much you had of land and rent,
Your length in clay's now competent.
A long war disturb'd your mind,
Here your perfect peace is sign'd.
Of what is't fools make such vain keeping?
Sin their conception, their birth, weeping:
Their life, a general mist of error,
Their death, a hideous storm of terror.
Strew your hair with powders sweet:
Don clean linen, bathe your feet,
And, the foul fiend more to check,
A crucifix let bless your neck.
'Tis now full tide 'tween night and day,
End your groan, and come away.

JOHN WEBSTER

Upon a Child that Died

Here she lies, a pretty bud,
Lately made of flesh and blood:
Who, as soon, fell fast asleep,
As her little eyes did peep.
Give her strewings; but not stir
The earth, that lightly covers her.

ROBERT HERRICK

Song

When I am dead, my dearest,
  Sing no sad songs for me;
Plant thou no roses at my head,
  Nor shady cypress tree:
Be the green grass above me
  With showers and dewdrops wet:
And if thou wilt, remember,
  And if thou wilt, forget.

I shall not see the shadows,
  I shall not fear the rain;
I shall not hear the nightingale
  Sing on as if in pain:
And dreaming through the twilight
  That doth not rise nor set,
Haply I may remember,
  And haply may forget.

CHRISTINA ROSSETTI

275

Wake all the dead!

Wake all the dead! what ho! what ho!
How soundly they sleep whose pillows lie low,
They mind not poor lovers who walk above
On the decks of the world in storms of love.
  No whisper now, nor glance can pass
  Through wickets or through panes of glass;
For our windows and doors are shut and barred.
Lie close in the church, and in the churchyard.
  In every grave make room, make room!
  The world's at an end, and we come, we come.

SIR WILLIAM DAVENANT

The Epitaph of Graunde Amoure

O mortal folk! you may behold and see
  How I lie here, sometime a mighty knight;
The end of joy and all prosperity
  Is death at last, thorough his course and might;
  After the day there cometh the dark night;
    For though the day be never so long,
    At last the bells ringeth to evensong.

And my self called La Graunde Amoure,
  Seeking adventure in the worldly glory,
For to attain the riches and honour,
  Did think full little that I should here lie,
  Till death did mate me full right privily.
    Lo what I am! and whereto you must!
    Like as I am so shall you all be dust.

Then in your mind inwardly despise
  The brittle world, so full of doubleness,
With the vile flesh, and right soon arise
  Out of your sleep of mortal heaviness;
  Subdue the devil with grace and meekness,
    That after your life frail and transitory
    You may then live in joy perdurably.

STEPHEN HAWES

A St Helena Lullaby

('*A Priest in spite of Himself*' – Rewards and Fairies)

'How far is St Helena from a little child at play?'
What makes you want to wander there with all the world between?
Oh, Mother, call your son again or else he'll run away.
(*No one thinks of winter when the grass is green!*)

'How far is St Helena from a fight in Paris Street?'
I haven't time to answer now – the men are falling fast.
The guns begin to thunder, and the drums begin to beat.
(*If you take the first step, you will take the last!*)

'How far is St Helena from the field of Austerlitz?'
You couldn't hear me if I told – so loud the cannon roar.
But not so far for people who are living by their wits.
('*Gay go up*' means '*Gay go down*' the wide world o'er!)

'How far is St Helena from an Emperor of France?'
I cannot see – I cannot tell – the Crowns they dazzle so.
The Kings sit down to dinner, and the Queens stand up to dance.
(*After open weather you may look for snow!*)

'How far is St Helena from the Capes of Trafalgar?'
A longish way – a longish way – with ten year more to run.
It's South across the water underneath a falling star.
(*What you cannot finish you must leave undone!*)

'How far is St Helena from the Beresina ice?'
An ill way – a chill way – the ice begins to crack.
But not so far for gentlemen who never took advice.
(*When you can't go forward you must e'en come back!*)

'How far is St Helena from the field of Waterloo?'
A near way – a clear way – the ship will take you soon.
A pleasant place for gentlemen with little left to do.
(*Morning never tries you till the afternoon!*)

'How far from St Helena to the Gate of Heaven's Grace?'
That no one knows – that no one knows – and no one ever will.
But fold your hands across your heart and cover up your face,
And after all your trapesings, child, lie still!

RUDYARD KIPLING

'Follow Me 'ome'

There was no one like 'im, 'Orse or Foot,
    Nor any o' the Guns I knew;
An' because it was so, why, o' course 'e went an' died,
    Which is just what the best men do.

So it's knock out your pipes an' follow me!
An' it's finish up your swipes an' follow me!
    Oh, 'ark to the big drum callin',
        Follow me – follow me 'ome!

'Is mare she neighs the 'ole day long,
    She paws the 'ole night through.
An' she won't take 'er feed 'cause o' waitin' for 'is step,
    Which is just what a beast would do.

'Is girl she goes with a bombardier
    Before 'er month is through;
An' the banns are up in church, for she's got the beggar hooked,
    Which is just what a girl would do.

We fought 'bout a dog – last week it were –
    No more than a round or two;
But I strook 'im cruel 'ard, an' I wish I 'adn't now,
    Which is just what a man can't do.

'E was all that I 'ad in the way of a friend,
    An' I've 'ad to find one new;
But I'd give my pay an' stripe for to get the beggar back,
    Which it's just too late to do!

So it's knock out your pipes an' follow me!
An' it's finish up your swipes an' follow me!
    Oh, 'ark to the fifes a-crawlin'!
        Follow me – follow me 'ome!

Take 'im away! 'E's gone where the best men go.
Take 'im away! An' the gun-wheels turnin' slow.
Take 'im away! There's more from the place 'e come.
Take 'im away, with the limber an' the drum.

For it's 'Three rounds blank' an' follow me,
An' it's 'Thirteen rank' an' follow me;
Oh, passin' the love o' women,
Follow me – follow me 'ome!

RUDYARD KIPLING

Complaint

If I was so soon done for,
What was I begun for?

ANON

A Ballade of Suicide

The gallows in my garden, people say,
Is new and neat and adequately tall.
I tie the noose on in a knowing way
As one that knots his necktie for a ball;
But just as all the neighbours – on the wall –
Are drawing a long breath to shout "Hurray!"
The strangest whim has seized me.... After all
I think I will not hang myself to-day.

To-morrow is the time I get my pay –
My uncle's sword is hanging in the hall –
I see a little cloud all pink and grey –
Perhaps the Rector's mother will *not* call –
I fancy that I heard from Mr Gall
That mushrooms could be cooked another way –
I never read the works of Juvenal –
I think I will not hang myself to-day.

The world will have another washing day;
The decadents decay; the pedants pall;
And H.G. Wells has found that children play,
And Bernard Shaw discovered that they squall;

Rationalists are growing rational –
And through thick woods one finds a stream astray,
So secret that the very sky seems small –
I think I will not hang myself to-day.

Envoi

Prince, I can hear the trumpet of Germinal,
The tumbrils toiling up the terrible way;
Even to-day your royal head may fall –
I think I will not hang myself to-day.

G.K. CHESTERTON

Do Not Go Gentle into that Good Night

Do not go gentle into that good night,
Old age should burn and rave at close of day;
Rage, rage against the dying of the light.

Though wise men at their end know dark is right,
Because their words had forked no lightning they
Do not go gentle into that good night.

Good men, the last wave by, crying how bright
Their frail deeds might have danced in a green bay
Rage, rage against the dying of the light.

Wild men who caught and sang the sun in flight,
And learn, too late, they grieved it on its way,
Do not go gentle into that good night.

Grave men, near death, who see with blinding sight
Blind eyes could blaze like meteors and be gay,
Rage, rage against the dying of the light.

And you, my father, there on the sad height,
Curse, bless, me now with your fierce tears, I pray.
Do not go gentle into that good night.
Rage, rage against the dying of the light.

DYLAN THOMAS

from *The Book of Common Prayer*

Man that is born of a woman hath but a short time to live, and is full of misery. He cometh up, and is cut down, like a flower; he fleeth as it were a shadow, and never continueth in one stay.

In the midst of life we are in death: of whom may we seek for succour but of thee, O Lord, who for our sins art justly displeased?

Yet, O Lord God most holy, O Lord most mighty, O holy and most merciful Saviour, deliver us not into the bitter pains of eternal death.

Thou knowest, Lord, the secrets of our hearts, shut not thy merciful ears to our prayer; but spare us, Lord most holy, O God most mighty, O holy and merciful Saviour, thou most worthy Judge eternal, suffer us not, at our last hour, for any pains of death, to fall from thee.

Then, while the earth shall be cast upon the Body by some standing by, the Priest shall say,

Forasmuch as it hath pleased Almighty God of his great mercy to take unto himself the soul of our dear *brother* here departed, we therefore commit *his* body to the ground; earth to earth, ashes to ashes, dust to dust: in sure and certain hope of the Resurrection to eternal life, through our Lord Jesus Christ; who shall change our vile body, that it may be like unto his glorious body, according to the mighty working, whereby he is able to subdue all things to himself.

Index of Poets

Index of Titles and First Lines

294